# BABYSPACE

## IDEA BOOK

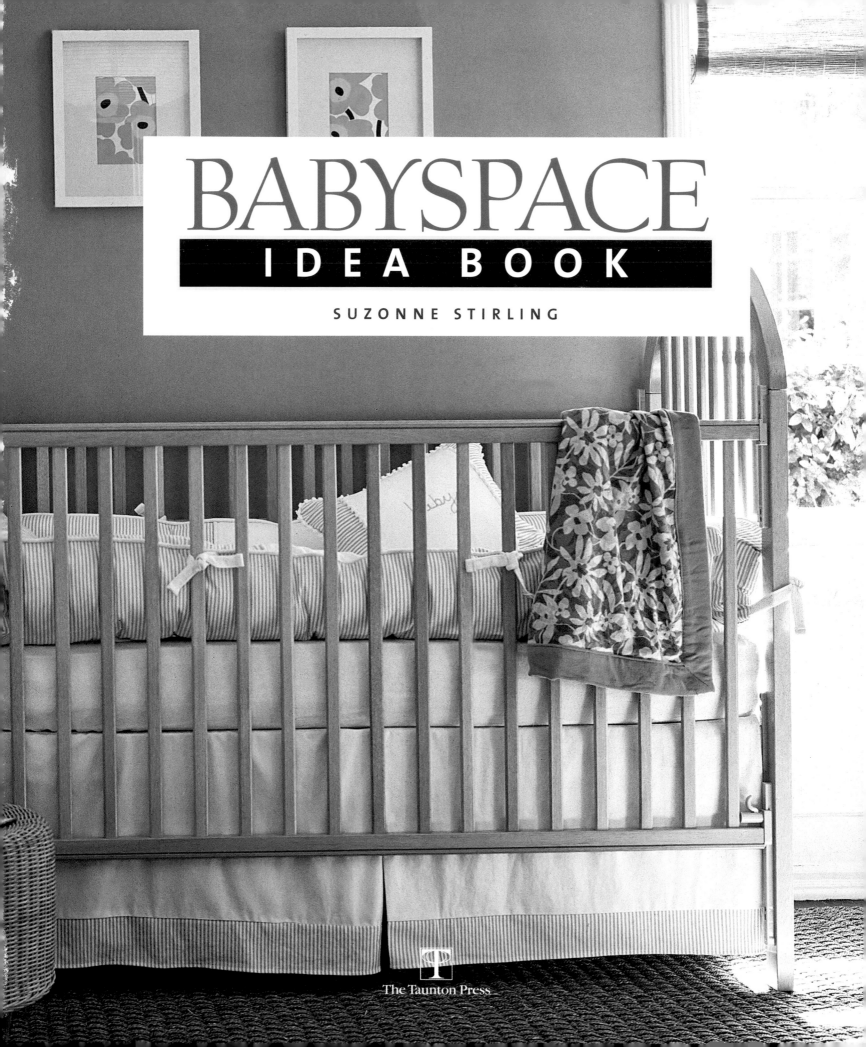

# BABYSPACE

## IDEA BOOK

SUZONNE STIRLING

The Taunton Press

**To Howard, who still believes in fairy tales**

© 2006 by The Taunton Press, Inc.

The Taunton Press
Inspiration for hands-on living®

The Taunton Press, Inc., 63 South Main Street, PO Box 5506, Newtown, CT 06470-5506
e-mail: tp@taunton.com

Editor: Stefanie Ramp
Interior Design and Layout: David Giammattei
Illustrator: Martha Garstang Hill
Front Cover Photographers:
    Top row, left to right: Photo © Lisa Romerein; Photo © Wendell T. Webber; Photo © Wendell T.
    Webber; Photo © Wendell T. Webber
    Middle row, left to right: Photo © Wendell T. Webber; Photo © Wendell T. Webber; Photo © Lisa
    Romerein; Photo © Wendell T. Webber
    Bottom row, left to right: Photo © Lisa Romerein; Photo © Mark Samu; Photo © Mark Samu;
    Photo © Wendell T. Webber
Back Cover Photographers: Top: Photo © Lisa Romerein; Bottom, left to right: Photo © Lisa Romerein;
    Photo © Chipper Hatter; Photo © www.stevevierraphotography.com

Taunton Home® is a trademark of The Taunton Press, Inc.,
registered in the U.S. Patent and Trademark Office.

Library of Congress Cataloging-in-Publication Data
Stirling, Suzonne.
  Babyspace idea book / Suzonne Stirling.
    p. cm.
  ISBN-13 978-1-56158-799-5
  ISBN-10 1-56158-799-0
  1. Nurseries. 2. Children's rooms. 3. Interior decoration. I. Title.

NK2117.N87S75 2005
747.7'7--dc22

                                            2005016190

Printed in the United States of America
10 9 8 7 6 5 4 3 2 1

The following manufacturers/names appearing in *Babyspace Idea Book*
are trademarks: Glidden®, Parcheesi®

# Acknowledgments

Like any birthing process, this book could only come about through the dedication and participation of many. I'd like to thank the photographers, architects, designers, and manufacturers who generously contributed their time, expertise, and talent to make this book a reality.

Thanks also to the excellent editorial and design team at The Taunton Press: Carolyn Mandarano, Stefanie Ramp, Jenny Peters, Wendy Mijal, and Julie Hamilton. I appreciate your guidance, patience, and support. Without you, this book would never have gotten off the ground.

On a personal note, I must thank my husband, Michael, whose unfailing support and encouragement in the face of deadlines, computer crashes, and frayed nerves make my creative life possible.

# Contents

# Introduction

The moment you cross the threshold of your home with a new baby, life as you know it is forever transformed: Your emotional world expands, you realize how much you're capable of with little sleep, and you find out just how much you have to learn. If it's your first child, this humbling experience is even more profound.

Your home and lifestyle go through a similar transition, as you're forced to examine your surroundings through a child's eyes, learning to baby proof as you go and swapping out an adults-only lifestyle for one that accommodates the little one in your life. And then there's the space factor, as mountains of baby gear suddenly show up in your cozy home once meant for two.

That's where *Babyspace Idea Book* comes in. It's filled with ideas to help make the transition a more comfortable one. There's no "one size fits all" approach here, but rather an understanding of the myriad challenges that new parents face, from creating a nursery to sharing their bedroom with an infant.

Like children, *Babyspace Idea Book* doesn't stop at infancy. It moves on to toddlers' rooms, with an emphasis on long-term design for parents living in today's overly busy world. The book also examines play spaces, honoring this important element of a child's development with cleverly designed rooms and hideaways that fully embrace the kids who create magic there. Then there's the rest of the house, where the focus is on making it a home for everyone, children and adults alike.

This book also tackles organizational challenges throughout the home, an important aspect of a pleasant and comfortable environment. Again, there's no single solution presented here, but rather a variety of ideas that anyone can incorporate into their existing floor plan.

Use *Babyspace Idea Book* to help you navigate your new lifestyle, inspire creative thought, develop long-term design strategies, and problem-solve. More important, use it as a foundation for your own unique style and a guide for bringing personal contributions to your home.

Welcome to a new world!

# Nurseries

Long before you decide on your baby's name, you will probably start planning her nursery. Perhaps you already have an extra room earmarked, complete with a mental image of the perfect nursery. Or you may be like most of us, trying to figure out how to make room for a new baby and feeling overwhelmed by furniture and color choices and all those baby names! So where do you begin?

The best way to get to know a room is to spend some time there. Judge the quality of light in the room, how the temperature relates to the rest of the house, and any awkward corners or areas of the room that need to be considered.

Once you've gotten a feel for the room, it's time to move on to choosing furniture. While practicality and safety should have top priority, you should also remember that creating a nursery isn't just a practical experience; you're preparing your heart and home for a momentous transition.

Enjoy the process. Open your mind to fresh ideas and new perspectives (good parenting advice, as well). Don't be afraid of color, feel free to shake things up, and welcome new life into your home.

◄ TEXTURE AND GENTLY COLORED ACCENTS keep a mostly white interior from feeling stark or sterile, as shown by this classic nursery. Detailed trim gives the room depth and prevents woodwork from blending in with the wallpaper, while subtle patterns in the rug add visual interest to the floor.

# Starting with the Basics

▲ INVESTING IN A COMFORTABLE ROCKING CHAIR may seem like a luxury, but it quickly becomes a neces- sity as late-night feedings take their toll on a weary parent. A plain storage cube with a painted interior becomes a charming decorative element as well as an impromptu tabletop.

N O MATTER WHAT THE CIRCUMSTANCES, most nurseries have four basic items: a crib, a changing table, a nursing chair, and some type of storage. These should be hardworking, well-made pieces. But besides being practical, each element can function as a building block for additional design. Find a piece of furniture you love and an entire room can be created around it.

Ultimately, your goal in designing a nursery is to create a functional, efficient space that feels warm and welcoming for your baby. It should also be a room *you* feel comfortable in. After all, a nursery is as much a parent's home in the first year as it is the baby's, perhaps more so.

So keep it simple. Keep it basic. But definitely let it reflect who you are and what you love.

▼ AN ALL-WHITE CRIB AND ACCESSORIES are soothing rather than bland, with a mix of textures and subtle color variations to engage the senses. The soft yellow of the wall enhances the natural light streaming into the room, giving it a warm, golden glow.

▲ STORAGE BECOMES DECORATIVE, not merely utili- tarian, with an eclectic assortment of containers stashed inside a simple wardrobe. Cheerful lined shelves and washable basket liners add charm and color, in addi- tion to being useful.

▲ THIS SIMPLE CHANGING TABLE comes with a removable cushioned pad. When baby gets older the pad can be removed and the piece used for toy storage. Wicker baskets keep clutter at bay and provide textural detail to a basic setup.

▲ PARING DOWN TO BASICS is a natural choice for enhancing the minimalist design aesthetic favored by these urban parents. The crib, with its traditional yet clean styling, easily harmonizes with adult furnishings and fixtures while the nursing chair, though modern in feel, curves around the body for comfort.

▲ THE CRIB TAKES CENTER STAGE in this nursery with its vivid bedding and prominent architectural design. A drop-latch side rail makes it easy for parents to reach inside of the crib, and the broad molding on both headboard and footboard prevents baby's clothing from getting caught.

▶ SUBSTANTIAL FURNITURE warms up the nursery and doesn't require much accessorizing. The pieces shown here are also good investments as the dresser can be used throughout childhood, while the crib will easily convert to a toddler bed in the future.

# Safety Basics

CREATING A HAZARD-FREE ENVIRONMENT should be a top priority. Planning your nursery with safety in mind will save time, money, and unnecessary stress later in the process.

- Keep a working smoke and carbon monoxide detector in or near the nursery.
- Cover all electrical outlets.
- Avoid floor-length curtains or drapes; a crawling baby can easily pull them down.
- Blinds with long cords are a strangulation risk. Install a cleat or hook high up on the window frame and loop cords around it, completely out of baby's reach.
- Gather and secure any electrical cords with a twist-tie.
- Install window guards on windows and make sure latches are secure.
- Make sure heavy toy boxes have safety hinges on the top.
- Avoid floor lamps, which are easily knocked over.
- Install radiator guards.

## CRIB SAFETY

- Use a crib with slats no more than 2³⁄₈ in. apart.
- Avoid cribs with cutouts in the headboards or footboards.
- Measure to be sure the top of the railing is at least 26 in. above the mattress.
- Beware of elevated corner posts on a crib; baby's clothing can get caught on them.
- Avoid cribs with easily released drop-side latches. Look for latches that require two distinct actions or a minimum force of 10 pounds with one action to release them.
- Make sure the mattress fits snugly in the frame.
- Keep pillows, comforters, quilts, and stuffed toys out of the crib. Remove the bumper once baby is able to pull himself to a standing position to prevent it from being used as a stepping stone.
- Never place a crib directly against a window; the sun is too strong for delicate skin, and baby may climb onto the windowsill.

▲ THIS RADIATOR COVER PROVIDES SAFETY while also serving as a decorative element that enhances the setting. The wide top can be used for extra storage.

## CHANGING TABLE SAFETY

- Purchase a table with a flat, wide surface to easily accommodate a growing infant; high side rails offer extra protection.
- Storage space is important. You'll need to keep one hand on your baby at all times; everything you need should be well within reach.
- You'll need a padded surface for the top of the changing table. Choose a thick, contoured, waterproof pad, preferably with a safety strap.
- Protect your back; purchase a table that's a comfortable height for you.
- A good table will be stable when shaken; if not, bolt it to the wall.

# Designing with Color

GONE ARE THE DAYS WHEN PARENTS SIMPLY PAINTED A ROOM pink or blue and called it quits. Today, color choices abound and parents are designing with an eye on the future. A pastel pink room can feel dated quickly, but take it up a few notches and you've got a color you can live with well beyond baby's first year.

Parents are also getting away from gender-specific colors and playing with strong, happy palettes that simply make kids feel joyful. It's a new, bright, colorful world and it's easy to get in on the fun. A couple of coats of paint and you've got a fresh makeover and a new outlook.

Another plus: More color allows you to get away with less accessorizing. And that's good for your budget!

▲ SMALL, SURPRISING DOSES OF COLOR can bring a neutral room to life. If vibrant wall color feels like too much of a commitment, pepper the nursery with lively accessories (like this switch-plate) that unify the room and provide stimulating focal points.

► A NEUTRAL, SUNNY YELLOW makes this room amenable to either sex and to a range of ages. A white crib keeps the look modern and fresh, while clever accents, like the shelf with hooks, message in letters above, and bright mobile, personalize the space.

▲ BOLD TONES GIVE THIS PAINT STAYING POWER, suitable far beyond infancy. The warm, bright pink provides an exuberant foundation with a decidedly feminine air. Details in the bedding and accents in the graceful furniture and accessories keep color center stage.

# RETHINKING PASTELS

▲ A SUCCESSFUL MIX of powerful color and strong graphic prints create a joyful nursery with a fresh, modern punch. Classic white furniture, softly colored bedding, and neutral flooring keep the combination exciting, not jarring.

▶ PALE PINK BEDDING mellows the bright orange of the walls and calms baby for sleeping. A mix of polka dots and stripes are fun, yet feminine when expressed in a soft palette. A ruffled bed skirt and blanket add a flirty touch.

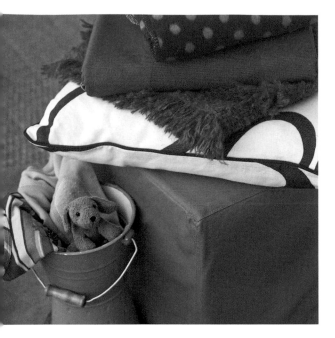

▲ MODERN GRAPHICS PAIRED WITH CLASSIC POLKA DOTS make a child-friendly statement in this nursery with its bold color scheme. Durable, crisp accents, such as the canvas ottoman and pillow, get softened by downy blankets, keeping the look warm and inviting rather than harsh.

# Improving Your Outlook

"THE PSYCHOLOGY BEHIND COLOR IS INCREDIBLY PERSONAL," says Barbara Richardson, color expert and director of color marketing for ICI Paints, maker of the Glidden® brand. "Adults have lifetime experiences they filter their perception of a color through. Their preferences come from strong emotional associations with the past, positive or negative experiences."

This is helpful to remember when you and your spouse simply can't agree on what color to paint the nursery. Delving beyond the personal, however, basic color psychology can help you create a room that's in harmony with your needs.

**Red:** Stimulates the appetite, heart rate, and breathing. Can make babies feel anxious, so it's better used as an accent color.

**Orange:** Associated with warmth and contentment; it's a nurturing color.

**Yellow:** Enhances concentration and stimulates learning, but it may make a baby cry more. It's the most eye-fatiguing color there is; if you're using it in a nursery, go softer rather than brighter.

**Blue:** Causes the opposite reaction as red. Relaxes the nervous system and has a tranquilizing effect, always helpful in a bedroom.

**Pink:** Calming; acts as a tranquilizer.

**Green:** The easiest color on the eye, it has a neutral effect on the nervous system; a serene, refreshing color.

**White:** Makes a room feel lighter and cooler.

◄ THINK OUTSIDE THE BOX when selecting paint colors for a nursery. Unexpected, saturated colors offer vibrancy and decorating longevity.

# UNIFYING WITH COLOR

▲ A FRESH APPROACH TO A TRADITIONAL COLOR gives this room a contemporary yet serene feel. Repeating the wall color in details throughout the room creates a feeling of cohesion, even with disparate furniture. An infusion of lime adds contrast and vibrancy.

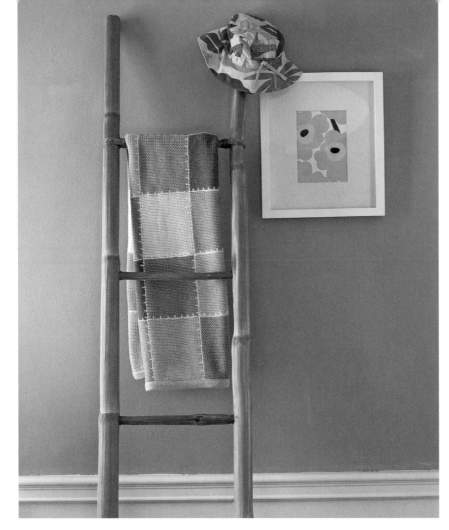

▲ WITH ITS HUES OF LIME AND TURQUOISE, this nursery feels inspired by nature. Nontraditional baby elements such as this bamboo ladder, pressed into service as a repository for blankets, reinforce the idea. The color scheme is further echoed in a swatch of fabric that's become art thanks to a simple frame.

## Problem Solving with Paint

Not a lot of light in the room? Use a warm color like yellow or gold. Does the nursery get intense light? Use cool or darker colors to manage some of that intensity.

Drawn towards a particularly strong color but don't want it on every wall? Consider a neutral paint for three of the walls and ceiling. Then paint one feature wall with the strong color. Later, if you tire of it, it's easy to repaint.

Looking to create a calming atmosphere? Paint the room in a single color. Adding another color, particularly a complementary one, creates more energy, so this might be a better choice for a playroom.

▲ AN OLD DRESSER benefits from a fresh coat of paint and contrasting knobs that pick up the hue from the walls. While currently doing double duty as a changing table, it's a solid transitional piece that will continue to be useful after baby is out of diapers.

▲ A STRONG, MODERN LAMP gets softened with stripes of aqua that bring it in line with the rest of the decor. It's an easy, do-it-yourself fix. Start with a basic opaque shade and use oil-based paint and masking tape to create your own complementary color accents.

# WALL TREATMENTS

▶ PALE PINK WALLS BECOME positively dreamy with the addition of floating bubbles painted over the basic wall color—an effect suitable for a baby but fully appreciated once she has grown a bit. This nursery furniture is adaptable for an infant or toddler, making it a good investment.

▲ NOT YOUR TRADITIONAL BABY PATTERN, this wallpaper marries a sophisticated stripe with a classic color scheme. The result is soft and ethereal, needing only ribbons and polka-dotted bedding to add a playful, youthful touch.

▶ CLASSIC RICKRACK ON THE BED SKIRT becomes a playful design element for this wall. Achieved with three colors of paint, it pairs beautifully with the vintage-style floral print of the linens, an effect both classic and fresh.

▲ A WHIMSICAL SCENE from a nursery rhyme was painted on this bedroom wall, becoming a strong decorative element. Supplemental storage is offered on the shelf, which blends seamlessly with the mural, creating a compelling focal point over the dresser.

◄ IN LIEU OF PAINTING OR WALLPAPERING, a moveable mural gives baby something to be stimulated by and delineates the nursery area in a shared room. A large canvas covered with fabric would work just as effectively as this painted canvas.

# Choosing Décor

ONCE UPON A TIME, designing a nursery was easy. Choices were limited. You started with pink, blue, or yellow. Maybe a lavender or mint green. Then you chose the bedding and baby accessories that fit conveniently into those color schemes, a ruffle for decoration, perhaps a stripe. One-stop shopping.

But parents slowly began to change the market, asking for products that were more stylish and appropriate for their home. This has resulted in color combinations that are more exciting, more sophisticated. Fabric patterns are fresh and fun, often without a baby motif. Furniture choices have expanded to include more streamlined and design-conscious pieces—an approach that gives the modern nursery longevity, making it appealing for older children as well.

Of course, you can still find traditional if that's what your heart desires. But it's also wonderful to have the option of mixing contemporary with traditional, of incorporating an eclectic mix that's a reflection of your personal aesthetic to create a room that truly embraces a new member of the family.

▲ A VINTAGE-STYLE CRIB with a sheer canopy is offset by fresh, modern floral bedding in a classic color scheme of pink and green. The subtle diamond pattern on the crib skirt adds visual interest to the floral bumper, a departure from the usual bedding sold in matching prints.

▶ CONTEMPORARY OPTIONS in furniture and bedding have expanded for style-conscious parents, as exemplified by this nursery with its nontraditional color palette and mixture of sophisticated and childlike elements. The tailored bedding feels clean and fresh, not babyish or cloying, a design choice that holds up over time.

# Feathering the Nest

THE CRIB IS MORE IMPORTANT TO YOUR BABY than any other piece of furniture in the nursery. A comfortable baby translates to a happy, sleeping baby, so vital in those first few months.

It's pretty simple to outfit a bed that meets your baby's needs. Select a firm mattress that fits snugly in the crib. Purchase fitted sheets that allow for shrinkage, as the elastic will need to fully cover the entire mattress. Purchase a bumper to protect baby's head until she can stand, and you're basically done.

But, oh, the fun you'll have when it comes to selecting bedding. An entire room can be fashioned around the crib, and modern options make it more fun than ever. Splurge, if you like. You deserve it. Because when it comes right down to it, adorable bedding is really just for mom and dad.

▲ ROMANTIC YET MODERN, this large, gregarious floral print is nursery appropriate in delicate shades of lilac and celery. A softly colored crib skirt adds to the romance.

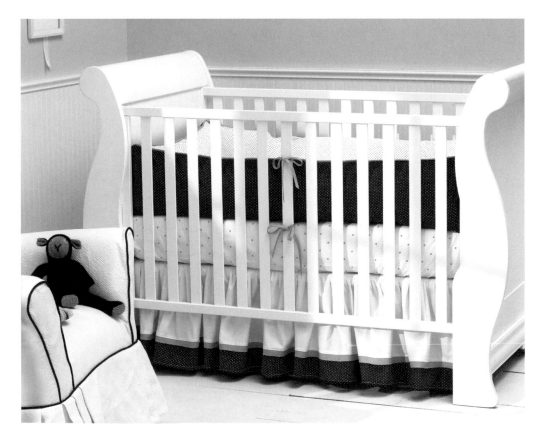

◄ CRISP NAVY-AND-WHITE BEDDING with a surprise hit of lime makes for a tailored, classic ensemble. Tiny polka dots add a sweet, childlike accent.

# UNIFYING THE DÉCOR

► WALL HANGINGS, PILLOWS, AND LAMPSHADES
are an easy way to create an informal theme in a
nursery. As your baby grows and interests change,
they're easy to swap out without starting from
scratch. Neutral furnishings allow for multiple rein-
terpretations of the room.

▼ A GROWN-UP COLOR SCHEME feels restful, while circus
motifs add a playful component. Patterned fabric pennants
and pillows are easy do-it-yourself accents that complement
the whimsical bedding. With decorating longevity in mind,
only the crib will need to be replaced in a year or two.

# Making the Most of Your Budget

UNLESS YOU PLAN TO REMODEL THE NURSERY **every few years**, you'll need to plan for the future right from the beginning. Your decorating dollars will best be spent on quality furniture that will adapt and last for years, such as a crib that converts into a youth bed or a changing table that can be used as a bookcase later.

Avoid age-specific design motifs in large parts of the room; choose timeless furnishings and wall treatments, then accessorize with baby items that can easily be swapped out. Forego wall-to-wall carpet in favor of area rugs that can be replaced when dirty or worn out.

When selecting accessories for the nursery, however, think beyond practical and opt for colors and patterns that you truly love. Gather photos for inspiration, along with color and fabric swatches. Sit with them for a while and you'll begin to see a pattern emerge, something you're drawn to over and over, whether a color or theme. Go with your instincts and you'll create a room you're happy to live with. And that's worth every penny you'll spend.

▲ BORROW A TRICK FROM DESIGNERS: Gather swatches and favorite objects for inspiration. Layer and rearrange until you find a combination that's visually compelling.

◄ THIS FORMER GUEST ROOM needed only the softening effect of pink to become suitable for a baby. Simple, graceful furniture and pale, solid fabrics offset the bold print of the wallpaper. Small touches of black unify the room without weighing it down.

► A BORDER ALONG THE TOP OF THE WALL
visually produces the sense of a cozy, intimate
space, as does the charming, casual furniture.
The pink crib is balanced by the white bookcase, which prevents the room from being
overwhelmed by rosy hues.

▼ WHIMSICAL AND TRADITIONAL PRINTS blend effortlessly
in this nursery, the plaid picking up hues present in the printed
fabric. Plaid, used sparingly, provides bold contrast. Fanciful
printed fabric used on the grown-up chair creates a whimsical,
child-friendly place for feedings, and later, bedtime stories.

# Light Up Your Life

THE QUALITY OF LIGHT IN A NURSERY is important. Too much direct sunlight can interfere with naptime. A street-light shining onto the crib at night poses the same problem. To alleviate such situations, make sure the crib is properly placed and windows fitted with blinds or shades.

Having minimal natural light in a nursery poses a different set of problems. It's excellent for sleep but can make the nursery feel heavy and, well, dark. In that case, you'll want to think of solutions to maximize what light there is. Use a pale sunny color, such as yellow, on the walls. Accent the room with table lamps, preferably with bulbs that simulate daylight. (However, you'll want to make sure that table lamps are out of reach when baby's old enough to pull them down.)

For every room, regardless of natural lighting, installing a dimmer switch on the overhead light is a worthwhile effort. It gives you the freedom to create the atmosphere you need at the time you need it.

▲ WHEN DEALING WITH AWKWARD AREAS such as skylights, the solution can easily become part of the décor. This skylight cover gives baby something to stimulate him visually, as well as allowing for total darkness when necessary.

◄ CHAIR-RAIL MOLDING creates an easy separation of paint and wallpaper, allowing the use of both and adding visual interest. The cheerful yellow energizes the pale, classic wallpaper, while the nursery colors are brought together in the old-fashioned rug, which gives the room a warm, cozy vibe.

▲ SMALL TOUCHES UNIFY A ROOM. Coordinating the fabric of a cushion with the fabric on a window shade creates a feeling of cohesion without being overly formal or stuffy. The knight theme feels classic rather than trendy, and the stenciled floor makes this traditional room more playful.

# Flooring for Comfort and Safety

**B**ABIES SPEND A LOT OF THEIR TIME ON THE FLOOR, especially once they've learned to crawl, so flooring has to meet high standards. It needs to be safe, comfortable for your baby, and easy for you to maintain.

Surprisingly, the safest surfaces are hard. Though it provides cushion, carpet also harbors allergens harmful to your baby. As for maintenance, hard floors are resilient and easier to keep clean. But where does that leave comfort?

A happy compromise is hard flooring, such as hardwood, accented with area rugs for both comfort and sound insulation. Rugs are easier to clean than carpet and easily replaceable if necessary. To add to their durability, consider using a fiber seal to repel spills and stains.

If you're looking for a clean, rather modern feel, sealed cork can work well in a nursery. It's sound absorbing, soft, and relatively easy to install. Of course, it too can be covered with a colorful area rug.

▶ A SOFT, NUBBY RUG is easy on baby's knees when crawling begins.

▲ MIXING PATTERNS isn't as tricky as it seems. You can freely mix florals with plaid and polka dots with stripes. Harmonizing the colors in each pattern allows for greater flexibility, even with busy prints. If your room is tiny, hang mirrors to visually enlarge the space as was done here.

▲ A TIMELESS ROOM, such as this one with its subtle wallpaper and classic furnishings, transitions easily from a nursery to a toddler's room. The canopy over the crib shades a sleeping baby from excessive light, while crib placement softens a sharp corner of the room, harmonizing it with its surroundings.

# THEMED ROOMS

▶ A PAINTED MURAL elongates this small room and draws the eye into the valley beyond. The trees in the mural make the ceiling seem higher, while fanciful creatures keep baby company.

▲ THIS SOOTHING NURSERY is knit together from country and nature themes. Buttery yellow walls bring in the sunshine and offset the deep greens and browns present throughout the room. Touches of soft white add a crisp note.

▲ A PAINTED DRESSER BECOMES A CANVAS for artistic expression. Parents who lack painting skills can achieve the same effect by decoupaging cutouts to the front of the drawers. Tone-on-tone paint—the complementary greens—lightens the overall look.

▼ THIS LITTLE ALCOVE becomes a storage power-house when outfitted with a custom-built window seat that doubles as a changing table. Additional storage cabinets underneath provide plenty of space for toys. Later, it will be the perfect reading nook.

▲ A SMALL, AWKWARD CORNER feels cozy instead of claustrophobic with the addition of a painted ceiling, which neatly fills in for an overhead mobile. A coordinated storage bag on the crib makes maximum use of space, as does the decorative shelf on the wall.

▶ A VINTAGE LAMP is the foundation for this nursery-rhyme theme, carried out by cheerful printed fabric throughout the room. Simple, striped fabrics on the table and chair provide contrast but harmonize effortlessly. The basic yellow walls will allow for an easy redesign of the room in years to come.

▲ A CLASSIC STORYBOOK THEME gets carried over to decorative accents such as the lampshade, miniature figurines in the cabinet, and the vintage watering can. The glass at the back of the cabinet creates a sense of depth while showing off the wallpaper and complementing the delicate contents inside.

▲ HEIRLOOMS AND HANDMADE GIFTS, such as this wall hanging/baby blanket, give a room personality. Display them instead of tucking them away in boxes. As baby outgrows such memorabilia, they can be archived for the next generation and replaced with more age-appropriate items.

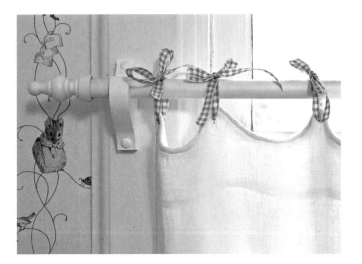

▲ INEXPENSIVE AND EASY do-it-yourself additions make the basics more exciting but still approachable and functional. Used in exacting ways, tiny patterned ribbons, like these gingham ones, stand out and create visual impact for a nursery window.

▲ BOLSTERED BY A STRONG DOSE OF WHITE, this whimsical wallpaper is still neutral enough to support strong patterns and colors in the room's fabrics. Surprising combinations, such as plaid and floral, mix readily and offer a traditional feel.

# SIMPLE THEMED ELEMENTS

▶ THE CRIB itself becomes both the focus of the room and an instant heirloom with the addition of customized touches. The rug and curtains are easily obtained, solid basics that nevertheless support the Western feel, while charming printed bedding fully expresses this classic theme.

▼ STRONG, GRAPHIC BEDDING creates a playful mood in this otherwise subdued room. A simple pennant is easily constructed from fabric remnants and further defines the circus theme, while the coordinated chair fabric and bed skirt feel nicely matched without being too fussy.

▲ VINTAGE-STYLE THEMED BEDDING makes a strong impact and provides a solid foundation, while touches of blue and an antique mobile further reinforce this simple theme. The rustic wood furniture and floor echo the naturalistic, country-cabin feel and serve as a unifying element.

◄ ONE SIGNATURE PIECE can give an entire room focus. This vintage stork, found at a flea market, allows the nursery to take on a vintage feel without much effort. If combined with contemporary styling, it becomes a whimsical note.

# Peel and Stick Art

IT CAN BE DIFFICULT TO COMMIT to a decorating scheme, particularly if you're a parent who craves change. Or perhaps commitment isn't your problem, but rather a self-perceived lack of artistic skill. In either case, peel and stick decals are an easy fix for a bare nursery or living space.

Decals come in borders, individual cutouts, and scenes, all with the ease of peel and stick application. Arrange a farm scene over a crib to create a focal point for the nursery, or use a decorative border over a changing table to distract your baby during diaper changes. Place designs around door frames or create patterned trim along the top of a wall.

Easily removed, decals won't strip paint or wallpaper and they can be rearranged countless times to satisfy your need for change or your inner perfectionist.

► PEEL AND STICK ART is perfect for a room meant to grow with your child. Swap out baby-oriented themes for more age-appropriate decals and you've got a versatile decorating solution.

# Sharing a Bedroom with Baby

NOT ALL NEW PARENTS FIND THEMSELVES in a spacious home with an extra bedroom suitable for a nursery. Some are city dwellers living in small apartments and unable to move to a larger space. Others work from home, so that extra bedroom has already been transformed into an office or studio.

Of course, those parents will need to find new solutions as their child grows. But what about the first year of life; is it truly necessary to have a complete nursery? Are there ways to successfully integrate a baby into an existing household without wholesale renovation?

There are. Undoubtedly, they require compromise, but solutions don't have to lead to unhappiness. Basically, pare your needs down to the essentials and get as organized as possible. In the end, you'll have less clutter to deal with and peaceful cohabitation—at least for a little while.

▼► PARENTS AND BABY CAN EASILY SHARE SPACE in the first months of life. The keys to peaceful cohabitation are simple, practical furnishings and a soothing palette. Organized storage keeps everything at hand while visually keeping chaos at bay.

▲ A SOPHISTICATED PALETTE of chocolate brown and warm, pale blue appeals to all ages. Classic childhood elements, such as this cuddly teddy bear, soften the crisp, modern graphics of the bed pillows, synthesizing the adult and child features of the room.

▲ A SIMPLE, SPARE ROCKER fits easily in tight spaces. A cushion and a blanket make nighttime feedings more comfortable, while an ottoman does double-duty as a table with the simple addition of a moveable tray.

# Creating Storage

BABIES COME INTO THIS WORLD WITH NOTHING and quickly accumulate more material possessions than their parents. There are seemingly endless numbers of onesies, socks, hats, diapers, and toys to contend with. And let's not forget all the gear that starts to creep in and take over your household!

The solution is, quite simply, proper storage. But think beyond walk-in closets; aside from the fact that your nursery may not have one, walk-ins keep everything hidden behind numerous doors. Exposed storage can be attractive as well as more accessible. Armoires can replace closets, and furniture such as changing tables can do double-duty as extra storage.

The bottom line is that you'll need even more storage space than you think you do. Children's possessions grow exponentially, and what seemed adequate in the beginning won't feel like much later on. Don't hesitate to create as much storage in a room as you possibly can. You'll need it.

▲ EXPOSED STORAGE CAN BE ATTRACTIVE with a diffusing element, such as the wire mesh front of this cabinet. Textured baskets and painted boxes further serve to tidy up storage and keep the overall look comfortable instead of cluttered.

▲ THIS SPARE BUT FULLY FUNCTIONAL changing table handles overflow from a small bedroom closet. Deep shelves store multiple outfits, while shelves and hooks placed above the changing table create a space for accessories and small keepsakes.

◄ STORAGE OPTIONS ARE ENDLESS in this nursery, with its large dresser, painted storage bench, and customized closet. The converted bookcase placed in the closet keeps items well organized while adding additional storage space on top.

▼ SMALL SPACES require efficiently used vertical storage. This narrow stand triples the storage space with removable pails that can hold everything from small toys to grooming supplies, hats, and shoes.

◄ IF HIDDEN STORAGE IS MORE YOUR STYLE, this convertible changing table offers curtains for hidden storage, which also soften the look of utilitarian furniture. Storage cubbies on the removable top keep small items handy. Later, the table can be used as a bookcase.

▲ A LAUNDRY BASKET outfitted with a decorative liner becomes an attractive abode for stuffed animals. Other toys requiring adult supervision are stored in a whimsically painted dumbwaiter with a safety latch.

◄ OPEN BINS MAKE BABY'S TOYS ACCESSIBLE while keeping them separate and less cluttered. Lining the bins with squares of oilcloth is not only a decorative touch; it makes cleanup from sticky fingers a cinch.

▲ A LARGE STORAGE UNIT keeps everything readily accessible. Dresser drawers provide ample room for clothing, and the lit space between drawers and shelves serves as a tidy changing area. Small cubbyholes store toys separately and in easy reach of baby.

▲ MOST PARENTS END UP with clothing their infants haven't yet grown into. Keep closets clutter-free by storing extra clothing in straight-sided wicker baskets, hidden under a bench or other piece of standing furniture. Baskets can be used later for extra toy storage.

▲ SIMPLE TEXTURES AND A COAT OF PAINT add to the charm of these exposed storage containers without detracting from their usefulness. Blankets can be rolled and stored in baskets, either solid or open, like this one, while clothing and bedding are better in bins that allow air to circulate.

▶ SMALL NURSERIES require creative storage solutions. In this room, storage is amplified with the use of wire baskets stored under the crib. The bed skirt just obscures the tops of the baskets, letting their texture shine but keeping the view clean, not cluttered.

▲ THE ADDITION OF RODS ON A CHANGING TABLE
creates hanging space for extra blankets and other large
items. Decorative flowerpots are an inexpensive solution
for holding small items, such as ointments and creams,
while an attractive basket keeps extra clothing nearby for
those inevitable accidents.

◀ A SMALL BEDROOM CLOSET becomes
a storage workhorse when fitted with customized shelves. Vertical storage promotes
maximum usage, while shelves under
hanging clothes keep clutter off the floor
and provide space for a laundry basket.
A small bottom drawer filled with toys
delights a curious baby.

# Making the Most of an Armoire

AN ARMOIRE IS ONE OF THE MOST VERSATILE pieces of furniture, particularly for a baby's room. Most come with a clothes rod and shelves, allowing hung and folded clothing items to be stored in the same place. Plus, the shelves closest to the floor can be outfitted with bins and baskets for baby to get into. Stuff these with soft toys or even socks and shoes, giving your baby her first experience at learning where to find and store things she'll want to use every day. Best of all, armoires come complete with doors, so that you can close up any mess quickly!

▲ WOODEN SOCK DRAWERS, painted to match the room's décor, are the perfect size for pint-size clothing. Use them to store rows of onesies or tiny shoes and socks, notorious for getting separated from their partners.

▲ WALLPAPER APPLIED TO THE BACK of this armoire brings unexpected charm to a functional piece. Shelves placed a bit lower than usual provide ample room for shoes and accessories to be stored underneath the hanging clothes.

▲ A HANGING ORGANIZER customized with colorful fabric remnants serves as a useful catchall. It doesn't take up much space, but is perfect for bibs, small toys and books, and other accessories you want to keep close at hand.

▲ FULLY OUTFITTED, this delightful armoire replaces a built-in closet. The small space is functional and efficient, with organized contents contained in boxes and bins. Storage on the doors maximizes every inch of space, while special toys and keepsakes can be displayed on top.

# Bedrooms for Toddlers

Toddlers are exuberant, exciting creatures. They're busy learning, exploring, and asserting their independence. They adore repetition, yet have short attention spans. They're imaginative, creative, messy, and full of energy. They can be, by turns, delightful then monstrous.

The best toddler rooms manage to cater to their ever-changing needs while providing a sense of stability and structure. Striking colors and patterns appeal to them visually, accessible toys and storage allow them control over their environment, and a cozy bed with a favorite friend or two helps the restless toddler settle down. Toddlers also appreciate plenty of floor space for free play, a reading area, a place for arts and crafts, and an area for dress-up and make-believe.

Fantasy is right at home in the toddler's room, too, because kids of this age group so easily move between what is real and what is imaginary. Murals, fanciful furniture, nooks, and hideaways all set the stage for grand adventures.

On a practical level, the best toddler rooms will grow and change as your child does. During these busy years, frequent redecorating will probably be less and less appealing. Crafting an easily transformable environment makes sense. Before you know it, your little toddler will be heading off for his first day of school!

◄ CREATIVITY IS ENCOURAGED with accessible zones for building, arts and crafts, and reading. Paint and simple patterns create a cheerful, coordinated suite of furniture. The bed is tucked into a corner, making it cozy and unobtrusive and allowing room for free play.

# Themed Rooms

B Y THE AGE OF THREE OR FOUR, children have distinct preferences and are generally able to communicate those desires, which means that they can participate in selecting themes for their rooms. Often, however, a toddler will want a room that focuses on an action figure or cartoon character he's grown to love. A couple of months and a full suite of themed accessories later, he's moved on to the next thing. Transcending the mass-market product blitz makes sense if you're looking to create an environment with staying power. That doesn't mean you shouldn't give in to a three-year-old's desires, but a printed pillow, themed lampshade, or large toy are often enough to satisfy his demands.

For longevity, the best themes are classic and easily adaptable. A room theme can be motivated by a color, the region the family calls home, a favorite pastime, a special heirloom, or a unique find—whatever creates a story and provides a haven.

▲ WHAT WAS ONCE A CHARMING NURSERY with a themed mural easily transforms into a toddler's room courtesy of a convertible crib. Simple wood furniture, taken from other parts of the house, blend easily in these storybook woods. The butterflies overhead add a colorful, tactile element.

► LIVELY PAINTED FURNITURE is an easy do-it-yourself project, even for those not artistically inclined. Simple patterns like stripes and checkerboards are created by blocking off areas with painter's tape. The pale yellow walls are a surprising and delightful background for this crisp, classic color scheme.

# Painted Effects

PAINT CAN WORK WONDERS IN A ROOM. Use it to design themes, create special effects and textures, enlarge a space or make it more intimate, or emphasize or deemphasize light. It's probably the most versatile and exciting tool you can invest in.

Think outside the box; paint the ceiling a different (but paler) color than the walls, quickly and inexpensively bring a shabby hardwood floor back to life, or create two-toned furniture.

If you feel intimidated by the idea of do-it-yourself painting projects, purchase paint and tools from a reputable home center and gather as much information from knowledgeable employees as you can. Before you know it, you'll be a pro.

▲ BOLD DOTS POP AGAINST YELLOW WALLS. Stencils were made from squares of easily removable, self-adhesive vinyl with circles cut out of the middle. Color was stippled onto the wall to minimize leakage under the stencil, and the stencil was removed after the paint had dried.

▲ A PAINTED WALL GETS A BIT OF TEXTURE with a dragging technique above the chair rail molding, achieved with a long, coarse-bristled brush. Bottom panels are accented with casually painted stripes.

◄ A PATTERNED BORDER painted directly onto the hardwood floor adds visual interest and structure to the open floor space. The design is sealed with floor sealer, protecting the paint and making cleanup a snap.

▶ A SPONGE-PAINTED BLUE GLAZE creates an ethereal ceiling with a soothing effect. Vintage accessories and simple furnishings keep the overall look light and clean and can be adapted easily as this child gets older. Plenty of open floor space gives him ample room to play.

▼ EVERYTHING'S SHIPSHAPE in a standard bedroom closet outfitted with customized drawers, shelves, and cubbyholes. Hanging rods have been placed closer to the floor for easier access, with room left over for toy storage.

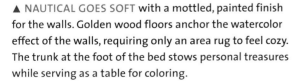

▲ NAUTICAL GOES SOFT with a mottled, painted finish for the walls. Golden wood floors anchor the watercolor effect of the walls, requiring only an area rug to feel cozy. The trunk at the foot of the bed stows personal treasures while serving as a table for coloring.

▲ THIS FANTASY ROOM leaves no stone unturned, with decorative painting on ceiling and walls and vibrant patterns everywhere. The look stays lively instead of overwhelming due to the liberal doses of white. Curtains hung from the bed frame create the illusion of an extra window.

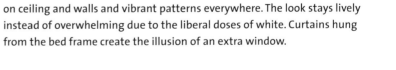

◀ PAINTED DRAWERS echo the vibrant colors found in the room's palette, colors that are stimulating and visually interesting to young children. Bug-themed knobs are an appropriate, whimsical touch for this garden bedroom.

▼ A FUNKY CHANDELIER was the source of inspiration for this vibrant and extravagant room, providing color and design clues. Unique finds provide a strong focal point for a themed room and create a personal, rather than mass-market, feel.

▼ A PAINTED BORDER above a picture rail makes a potent impact in this room without weighing it down. A similar effect can be achieved with a wallpaper border and is easily replaced as your child grows. Details like the zebra-print lamp add to the fun.

► NO DETAIL IS OVER-LOOKED in this exuberant jungle room. A grown-up bed is balanced by the whimsical table and chairs meant only for child's play. A long window seat encourages animal exploration, while deep drawers hold the accoutrements of adventure.

▲ A DEEP-RED WALL provides a dramatic backdrop for this nautical theme. Open windows suffuse the room with natural light and prevent the red from feeling heavy. White furnishings, ceilings, and trim keep the overall effect crisp and graphic, while cheerful fabrics add a playful note.

► A SOOTHING MURAL DRAWS THE EYE beyond the boundary of the wall, making this room appear larger. Sandy, neutral carpeting and walls complement the sea theme, while shades of blue are echoed in the furniture and accents. A simple bookcase also makes a handy nightstand.

▲ ADULT FURNISHINGS GET A MAKEOVER fit for a knight. A basic bookcase gets a *trompe l'oeil* treatment, and a decorative wooden cutout mounted to the wall creates a compact headboard. A game table awaits future chess matches, while the open floor space and low-weave carpet provide a solid surface for toddler play.

# Themes on a Budget

THEMES CAN EASILY BE CREATED THROUGH ACCESSORIZING ALONE. The bed frame, nightstand, overhead shelf, and neutral rug are common to all of the rooms shown here, but simple, minimal details completely change the tone of each room, demonstrating how easy it will be to reinvent in the future.

The key is to invest in bold elements that make a powerful impact in a basic room. Patterned bedding creates a strong focal point. A few well-chosen themed items placed close to the bed easily reinforce the idea, as groupings of like items tend to make more of an impact than small pieces on their own.

Another idea is to create a themed corner, especially if your child has her heart set on something that will quickly become dated. Create a charming reading nook with a themed lampshade and chair cushion along with relevant books. It's a budget-conscious solution you'll both be able to live with.

▲ THE SMALL AREA RUG punches up neutral flooring and makes a strong statement. The bedspread and blanket echo the colors found in the rug, while a printed sheet and pillowcase create a distinct theme. Framed robot prints tie the look together, as does the robot collection on display.

▲ THEMED BEDDING CREATES A STRONG FOCAL POINT for this rodeo bedroom, while the lampshade, clock, and bedside frame are tied in with additional vintage-style western fabrics.

▲ VIBRANT FLORAL BEDDING accessorized by a backdrop of mod dots and a flower-themed lamp create a girlish room that's stylish, not overly sweet.

# Multiuse Bedrooms

ANY HOMES DON'T HAVE SPACE FOR A DEDICATED PLAY-ROOM, making a toddler's bedroom the center of her universe. It's here that she sleeps, plays, perhaps watches television, reads, builds, engages in arts and crafts, and entertains playmates.

Organized storage plays a starring role in the multiuse bedroom, especially toy storage, which should be easily accessible for a child. Toddlers tend to feel frustrated when they're unable to reach something by themselves, and it's easier for a parent to teach a toddler how to help clean his room when there are specific areas for toys and other belongings.

Another consideration is how to set up activity zones within a room; furniture that does double duty can help. A headboard bookcase easily combines the sleeping and reading area. A small table can double as a building zone and a place for coloring or drawing. If possible, it's also nice if at least part of the flooring is composed of something easily cleaned. That way, children can finger paint or play with modeling clay without incident.

▲ A WINDING BEACH PATH in the mural is echoed in the flooring, creating the illusion that it continues into the room, complementing this long, narrow space. The built-in platform is equipped with multiple drawers for toy storage, while the bed frame is replaced with multilevel shelving and built-ins.

► A CHEERFUL TEEPEE BECOMES A CLEVER HIDEAWAY within this bedroom. Uncovered windows bring in light and integrate nature with the simple, earthy furnishings. The bold use of color on the teepee and wall accents infuses energy into the neutrals that dominate most of the room.

◄ A SMALL BEDROOM BECOMES SPACIOUS with the construction of a loft, placed in front of a window for extra light. Steps lead to the bed, protected by decorative railings. Vertical storage uses space efficiently, leaving room for a special hideaway under the loft and a cozy reading corner.

▼ BUILT-INS MAKE USE OF AWKWARD SPACE in this small bedroom, with shelving that follows the sloping line of the ceiling, maximizing vertical space. A window seat provides extra play space as well as storage, while a bookshelf nestled against the footboard keeps toys close at hand.

▲ STORAGE OPTIONS ABOUND in this multiuse room. Storage steps built in behind the bed serve as both a headboard and a play area. Sliding covers make books and toys easy to access and easy to tuck away. A reading light encourages bedtime stories.

▲ PAINTED CABINETS, BOLTED TO THE WALL, easily become part of the décor with a bit of paint and also keep clutter at bay. Overturned paint cans make clever chairs for a kid-size table, and the faux-stone floor disguises smudges and dirt, making it perfect for a rough-and-tumble kid.

▲ OFFERING AMPLE SPACE FOR SELF-EXPRESSION, fabric-covered cork squares allow for an ever-changing personal tableau. Cherished memorabilia can be kept safe near the top, while bottom squares give a toddler his own exhibit space.

ROOM TO GROW

# From Babyproofing to Childproofing

YOUR TODDLER STILL NEEDS THE SAFETY PRECAUTIONS that were put into place when he was an infant. However, there's a new problem to contend with. Toddlers are constantly moving; they love to run and jump, and they especially love to climb. To ward off accidents, secure high dressers and bookcases to the wall.

Toddlers are also notorious for jumping on the bed. Make sure the bed isn't placed too close to a window and that all windows have safety guards and security latches.

▲ CLEVER BUILT-INS ADD SPACE to a small room. Fold-down tables provide play surfaces, with toys and games stored in the cabinets. When tables are folded up, padded seats with storage drawers underneath provide a comfy place to read or daydream.

▲ TUCKING THE BED INTO A BUILT-IN ALCOVE greatly expands this narrow room, creating space for play. A built-in shelf under the window becomes a handy desk or craft area. The painted mural enhances the simple, easily adaptable décor, adding visual interest and a focal point.

▲ STORAGE OPTIONS ABOUND in this room, with tall cabinets for hanging clothes and shelves for toys and books. Large, deep drawers under the windows hold more clothing, while additional toy storage is provided under the bed, which is built on a platform with stairs helpful for little feet.

## CLUTTER BUSTERS

# The Well-Designed Closet

CHANCES ARE THE CLOSETS IN YOUR HOME are sized for an adult, which leaves lots of unused space if not reconfigured. A standard adult closet comes with a hanging rod at the top and perhaps a shelf above that—not the most efficient design when you're dealing with small hanging clothes.

To maximize closet storage, determine how many hanging rods you really need to house clothes comfortably, then consider installing double rods or hanging a single rod closer to the floor. Once those are in place, add shelves, drawers, or hanging organizers to other parts of the closet; all are readily found in home improvement stores and are easy to install yourself.

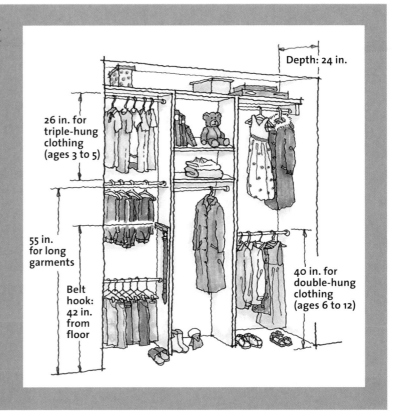

Depth: 24 in.

26 in. for triple-hung clothing (ages 3 to 5)

55 in. for long garments

Belt hook: 42 in. from floor

40 in. for double-hung clothing (ages 6 to 12)

# When Toys and Clothing Cohabitate

WHEN TOYS AND CLOTHING SHARE THE SAME CLOSET, **orga-nized storage is the key to parents' happiness.** Everything should have its own space, as much as is possible. Colored stacking drawers and bins make use of vertical space and allow children to help you clean up. You can make a game out of it by emphasizing the different colors of the bins and showing what belongs in each one.

Hooks, shelves, hanging organizers—they'll all help in a multiuse room. If the bedroom closet is large enough, outfit half of it with clothing, utilizing all vertical space in that half of the closet. Then do the same with the other half, but stock it with toy storage. Keep age-appropriate toys at child level; store toys that require supervision higher up.

If your closet isn't large enough, try storing clothing along the upper level and add low storage items along the bottom to stow toys.

▲ HANGING SHOE BAGS WITH CLEAR FRONTS help children find their own shoes without hassle; hooks attached to the closet door offer extra storage in an unexpected place.

▲ COLORFUL PLASTIC ACCESSORIES help keep parents and toddlers organized. Plastic's a good bet for toys and art supplies, since cleaning it is a cinch. Stackable bins are easily removed from the closet during playtime, while labeled boxes help parents determine contents without removing lids.

▲ HANGING SHELVES ARE MARKED with the weekdays, while outfits for each day are already in place. Double hanging rods make use of vertical space in this well-organized closet and clear the way for toy storage.

# Shared Rooms

Learning to peacefully cohabitate with others is something every member of the family contends with; learning to share a bedroom, however, is even more challenging. To ease the inherent conflict, a shared bedroom should include separate but equal space for both children. In short, both children should feel like they got the best part of the room. Providing equal storage, display space, and decorative elements can help head off discord.

However, most shared rooms house children of different ages, and what might be appropriate for one age isn't always appropriate for the other. If one of your children is old enough to utilize a desk, provide one for her and give your toddler a small table that she can use for coloring. If one has storage space under the bed, make sure the other has storage over the headboard. Each child then has equal but different components.

▼ HARDWOOD FLOORS ARE PAINTED in the same pale palette as the rest of the room, adding to the breezy feel. High-gloss porch paint makes cleanup a snap, while the simple design adds visual interest.

◄ NATURAL LIGHT REFLECTS off of this pale palette, creating a feeling of spaciousness. Décor is deliberately spare, contributing to a sense of serenity, while the comfortable chairs and storage ottoman create an intimate space for games and reading. Patterned seats and bedding prevent the room from looking too sterile or grown-up.

▲ WHEN CHILDREN SHARE A SMALL ROOM, efficient storage helps keep the peace. Tall, twin bookshelves provide individual areas for displaying books and special items, while ample drawer space keeps clothing separate. Additional drawers (one for each child) under the window seat hold toys.

▲ RETRO STYLING AND A CLASSIC BASEBALL MOTIF create a comfortable room that's coordinated but not stuffy, suitable for brothers with an age gap. The storage headboard on the top bunk keeps prized possessions away from a curious toddler, while small toys are easily stored under the bottom bunk.

▲ A FANCIFUL DRESSING AREA is designed with longevity in mind. Separate cabinets keep the peace between sisters, while the communal dressing table allows plenty of space for dress-up and makeovers. Additional cubbies overhead display faithful friends.

▶ DECORATED IN A BOLD PALETTE, this room is ageless. Iron bed frames take up less space than a bulky wood type would and keep the emphasis on color. The demitable bolted to the wall creates a sense of separation, while the overhead cornices lend a royal touch. Full bed skirts hide underbed storage.

▲ THIS CONVERTED ATTIC SPACE easily lends itself to sharing. Simple and clean, each side mirrors the other. The pair of windows provides equal light, while the cozy bench serves as communal space. Cleverly placed tables work as nightstands or set the stage for a tea party.

◄ SIMPLE, STREAMLINED FURNITURE and a large, well-placed window and skylight keep this tiny converted attic room from feeling claustrophobic. The small window seat makes a cozy niche to curl up in, with a view of the sky overhead. A low-pile rug allows comfortable floor play.

▲ A STURDY BUT DECORATIVE
SIDE RAIL protects a wiggly
sleeper, while the patterned
bedspreads add a needed burst
of color. Heavy, painted furniture suits rowdy boys; it's balanced by pale, subtly patterned
walls that reflect light, adding a
sunny glow.

▲ A PAINTED FLOOR BORDER with a Parcheesi®
game at the corner adds visual interest and complements the pattern of the bedroom rug. Different
game boards are painted in the other corners of
the room.

▲ SATISFYING A CHILD'S WHIM, a favorite book and
television character graces a high, heavy dresser that's
bolted to the wall for safety. While fitting for now, it
can easily be repainted when the infatuation wanes.

▲ A PALETTE OF COOL BLUE AND PALE YELLOW accented by happy bursts of red appeals to a toddler's love of color. Curtains over each headboard create an atmosphere of privacy, while individual benches give each child some personal space. Communal items, such as the train table, encourage shared play.

◄ EASY, PAINTED CANVASES can make a big impact and provide a punch of color where needed. Create your own art by painting simple patterns onto canvas or by using stencils and a ruler if your freehand style isn't to your liking.

▲ CHILDREN HAVE FREE REIN in what had been unused attic space. The unique architectural lines of the room mesh easily with the casual décor. Beds are tucked away under the ceiling vault, with a separate area for reading, movies, and play.

▶ A CUSTOM-BUILT PLATFORM affords privacy as well as storage in this small space. A divided closet takes up half the platform, while the other half houses a bed with a headboard shelf for personal possessions. A divided bulletin board gives each child a place to exhibit special items.

# A Note about Bunk Beds

**B**UNK BEDS ARE INVALUABLE IN A SHARED ROOM; **they make efficient use of floor space and allow kids a sense of separation. Top bunks aren't for toddlers! However,** your toddler can sleep on the bottom bunk if you have children of different ages sharing a room—if you have twins, wait on the bunk beds until they're at least six.

As always, safety is an issue. Buy a bed with protective railings on the top bunk for young children, and make sure the mattress is securely fastened to the bed.

▶ MANY BUNK BEDS are available with a protective railing incorporated into the design. Check to make sure it's sturdy and covers most, if not all, of the length of the bed.

▼ TONE-ON-TONE BLUE with accents of red and white create an uplifting color scheme. The starry sky overhead complements the recessed lighting, and even the ceiling fan seems like a natural part of the décor. Area rugs add a touch of color and design to the neutral carpeting.

▲ A BUILT-IN BED MAKES USE OF AWKWARD SPACE, creating a cozy niche that feels private, even in a shared room. Drawers under the bed offer a safe hiding place for storybooks and treasured possessions. The pint-size closet keeps toys out of sight.

▲ KIDS LOVE PERSONALIZED ITEMS, and with customized chairs there's no argument over what belongs
to whom. A small trunk works as a side table, keeping a
lamp at child level, while the comfy kid-size chairs pro-
mote reading and conversation. A handmade, fabric-
covered memo board provides space for keepsakes.

▲ A GENEROUSLY SCALED ROOM provides multiple comforts for
bunkmates. The rough-hewn beds include clever accents like the built-in
night table and underbed drawers. A daybed works as a place to relax
and watch television or host sleepovers in the future.

▲ COMFORT AND COLOR ARE KEY in this warm and vibrant bedroom. The textured wall color resembles washed
denim, while punches of red liven things up. A hand-me-down rug feels right at home in the reading area, warming
up the neutral carpet. Rope accents add a playful note.

# Sharing a Room with Baby

SOMETIMES SHARING A ROOM WITH A SIBLING is the only option when a new baby comes along. The greatest dilemma is often space. To make the most efficient use of space, try limiting nursery furniture to a crib, a changing pad on top of a dresser, and an area for storage. If there isn't a nursing chair already in the room, consider having one in another room where you won't wake up your toddler during late-night feedings.

Of course, safety precautions must be in place for both ages, and when your new baby is old enough to crawl you will probably need to move your toddler's small toys into a family room or make sure the baby is never left alone in the bedroom. Safety gates can help in this arena.

As far as décor goes, consider timeless options without baby motifs. Pastels work fine in a shared room, especially when punched up with brighter accents scattered around for more impact. Also think about giving greater weight to the toddler's desires, as your newborn won't care what color or style dominates the room.

▼ BATHED IN PINK, this room is girly but not babyish, with bright pink accents amping up the overall décor. Simple white frames for both the twin bed and the crib keep the room from looking overly crowded while unifying the furnishings. A tea table gives a toddler some space of her own.

◄ A TRADITIONALLY BOYISH COLOR SCHEME mixed with a floral border and oversized gingham curtains and bed skirt nicely bridges the gender gap in a room shared by a baby boy and his older sister. The dark bed frame visually separates the bedroom area from the nursery area.

# Furnishings

NEVER BEFORE HAS THERE BEEN so much furniture designed especially for children: small tables and chairs, diminutive bookcases, and fantasy furniture resembling everything from castles to tree houses. Children love this kind of furniture; it gives them permission to play and makes them feel right at home in their house.

However, scaled-down kids' furniture should be balanced with larger pieces in a room. Chairs and tables can easily be swapped out for larger pieces when your child has grown; an entire suite of small furniture, however, makes for a very expensive renovation.

When selecting fantasy furniture, opt for a classic theme your child can live with for a few years. Such pieces are rarely inexpensive, so you'll want to choose wisely. Another option is to decorate basic furniture with a painted motif that reflects your child's current passion. When your child outgrows the design, a fresh coat of paint provides instant transformation.

▲ OVERSIZE KNOBS ARE PERFECT for a toddler's clumsy grasp, while their whimsical design and color liven up a plain dresser. Later, they can be easily replaced by more age-appropriate hardware.

► A PINT-SIZE STORAGE BENCH makes a private reading area suitable only for a child. Fanciful wall painting makes seating appear even more diminutive; the oversize orchid on a tiny chair contributes to the Alice in Wonderland effect.

► THIS ROOM FEATURES A REPLICA of mom and dad's reading area, but it's just the right fit for their young son. The bookcase is scaled down to work with the small club chair. A table lamp above is set out of reach of a toddler's curious hands while still shining light onto storybooks.

▼ A WHIMSICAL, CLEVERLY DESIGNED TRAIN BED isn't just for show; it's a storage power-house, with a toy box built into the front, head-board shelves that hold petite passengers, and a side cabinet for stowing small treasures. Now, the trundle bed protects a toddler who may fall out of bed, but it will be useful for overnight guests later.

▼ A STRAY CHAIR TAKES ON NEW LIFE in a toddler's room. The bars make it easy for a little one to get a foothold, while the padded cushion provides comfort and protection from hard edges and also adds a youthful touch.

▲ THIS VERSATILE STORAGE HEADBOARD offers something to occupy your little one when sleep isn't an option. A safety rail keeps overhead books from tumbling down, and small cubbies provide a safe haven for a few sleeping buddies.

▲ A COZY BUILT-IN forms an enveloping nook for a small child. A mounted reading light encourages bedtime stories, while underbed drawers contribute to storage.

▲ SEPARATE PIECES OF FURNITURE look substantial when grouped together. Individual storage units bookend the desk, perfect for a room shared by two. The desk can accommodate two chairs, if needed, for side-by-side play. Later, it'll make a good study area.

# Fun with Paint and Decoupage

PAINTED FURNITURE IS PERFECT FOR KIDS' ROOMS; it's an easy way to add texture, pattern, color, and a touch of whimsy. It's also a good way to rescue thrift store finds or household furniture well past its prime.

Though it may look intimidating, even a novice can paint furniture. Take the minimalist approach and paint an old dresser a solid color, then add colorful hardware. Utilize painter's tape to create stripes, checks, or plaid. Use stencils for perfect polka dots or a more difficult pattern.

Decoupage also works well with painted furniture: Decoupage wallpaper remnants to the fronts of dresser drawers; apply patterned paper silhouettes to chairs or a simple bed frame.

For durability, sand furniture, if necessary, then prime with a latex primer followed by the paint of your choice. For best results, use semigloss enamel paint. If you're decoupaging, apply the desired cutouts to painted furniture with decoupage medium, then seal the entire area with more.

▶ ALL THE PIECES SHOWN HERE started out as unfinished furniture or lackluster finds at a yard sale. Spruced up with paint, decoupage, and decorative hardware, they rival more expensive customized furniture found in select boutiques.

# Places to Play

C hildren need to play. It's how they learn to use their imaginations, how they become socialized individuals, develop interests and hobbies, and begin to problem-solve. To fully enhance play, children need space to roam and explore. At the same time, they're drawn to enclosures, places to reflect and contemplate or create fantasy worlds. Whether it's a fully outfitted playroom or a hideaway tucked into an unused closet, children enjoy rooms that are meant for them—sized for them, decorated for them, and geared to handle their messes.

Ultimately, play is a state of mind. When children feel safe and secure in their surroundings, their imaginations are free to take flight. Whatever space you carve out for your children to play in, make it comfortable and safe, forgiving and flexible. Many types of play take place in a home over the years. Create play spaces with potential for growth and your children will return to that place of comfort and freedom over and over—eventually with friends in tow.

If you get stuck trying to think of creative ways to make space for play, ask your kids. Some of their desires will sound familiar. After all, the need for play never changes.

◀ FRAMED ARTWORK AND KID-SIZE FURNITURE create a room tailor-made for kids. The paneling is painted with semigloss paint for easy cleanup of stray crayon marks and smudges; the sealed stone floor is durable and neutral enough to adapt as kids' tastes change.

# Playrooms

A GREAT PLAYROOM IS A HAPPY PLAYROOM. Cozy or expansive, colorful and bright, it's a place for games, magic, make-believe, and art. Extra bedrooms, basements, unused attic space, converted walk-in closets or hallways all have the potential to become great playrooms.

Another trick to a great playroom is creating a space that's geared specifically toward your child's needs. Choose scrubbable paint or wallpaper for the walls and kid-friendly flooring that's easy to clean. Purchase furniture that's comfortable and durable, nothing you'll fret over if it gets marked up. Provide spaces for self-expression, whether by coating a wall with chalkboard paint or hanging rolls of drawing paper. Give them accessible storage and a place to put everything away. If at all possible, incorporate a little hideaway, perhaps a reading alcove, an indoor playhouse, or a portable teepee.

It also helps if you can think like a child. What did you once love? Chances are your child will enjoy much of the same.

▲ SLIDING DOORS COATED WITH A DRY-ERASE SURFACE create two separate playrooms for siblings of different ages, while a cutout in the door keeps them visually connected and allows light to filter through. A cement floor coated with high-gloss paint is perfect for this high-traffic area, and area rugs give kids a soft place to sit.

▶ A FINISHED BASEMENT becomes a full-service playroom with its separate kitchen and various activity areas. Kid- and adult-size furniture mingle easily, while plenty of accessible storage keeps the room open and spacious. A black rubber floor mat makes for easy cleaning and hides stains.

# Making a Splash

A PLAYROOM IS A GREAT PLACE TO EXPERIMENT WITH COLOR. Basically, anything goes. Paint every wall a different color, use bold shades you wouldn't consider using in other parts of the house, paint trim in unusual combinations, mix different colors of furniture, or go for brightly colored slipcovers. This is the place to really let your inner artist run wild.

Children respond to color. It invigorates them and stimulates their imaginations, just as it does for adults. Color in a playroom invites them to create masterpieces, invent grand adventures, and feel alive and exuberant. Just what you want in a playroom.

Color has an advantage for parents as well. Bold color and cheerful patterns disguise dirt and stains better than pale ones do, an important consideration in a playroom, where many different messy activities take place.

▲ A COLORFUL, PRIMITIVE JUNGLE MOTIF disguises clever storage and display strategies. Stuffed animals lurk behind a wooden screen, while recessed bookshelves offer additional toy storage. Flat fiberboard trees are actually display space meant for children's artwork, and vinyl flooring incorporates a game board into the décor.

▲ UNABASHED USE OF COLOR transforms this simple bedroom into a bright and cheery playroom with easy cleanup potential. The high-traffic portions of the lower walls are coated with semigloss paint, while the upper walls are painted with matte latex paint. The vivid paint job on the doors and trim helps disguise fingerprints and scuff marks.

▲ A CHILD'S VERSION OF HEAVEN, this indoor playroom provides direct access to the backyard, making it suitable for hours of play. Brightly colored accents add a playful note to this modern, soaring space, with windows overlooking the space allowing for supervision when necessary.

# Flooring That Doesn't Play Around

IN HIGH-TRAFFIC AREAS LIKE A PLAYROOM, floors need to be durable and low maintenance. Instead of wood or carpet, consider cork, vinyl, linoleum, or rubber.

Cork is comfortable underfoot, comes in various stains, and can be finished with easy-to-clean urethane. Vinyl, a cinch to vacuum or mop, is available in myriad colors and designs. Linoleum, an old favorite in the kitchen, works well for the "wet side" of a playroom, where arts and crafts take place. Rubber flooring is inexpensive, sound insulated, and naturally slip-proof. And there's always the low-tech route: Use drop cloths to temporarily protect as needed.

▶ CREATE ACTIVITY AREAS IN LARGE SPACES to help old and young kids play together in harmony. Here, open shelving and closed storage units provide ample space for books, toys, and craft and art supplies. Two desks define space for computers and homework. Plenty of floor space allows kids of all ages to move around. If your space has stairs, like this one, consider a gate to keep toddlers safe.

▲ OPEN SHELVING SERVES AS A ROOM DIVIDER, handily separating activity zones while providing lots of storage. One side acts as a study area for older children while the other is more suitable for a toddler. A mounted ladder on a horseshoe rail allows access to items stored on high shelves.

◄ UNUSED ATTIC SPACE is easily transformed into a playroom with a bright splash of color and activity zones that conform to the lines of the room, such as the lounging area built in under the eaves. Low ceilings are balanced by kid-size furniture, making it a comfortable fit for the little ones.

# TRANSFORMED SPACES

▲ A CONVERTED HALLWAY BECOMES A CHEERFUL PLAY-ROOM connected to a child's bedroom. High-density natural cork flooring is easy to care for, comfortable to play on, and sound-insulated. Cool, beautiful colors enhance the narrow space, making it seem larger, while windows between the hallway and bedroom provide light and visual flow.

◄ A FINISHED ATTIC BECOMES A HANDY ROOM for arts and crafts. The beadboard walls, covered in bright semigloss paint, make cleanup easy, as do the added sink and laminate cabinets. Window guards keep children safe while letting in natural light.

# Think Outside the (Toy) Box

CHILDREN DON'T REQUIRE FANCY PLAY-ROOMS TO MAKE THEM HAPPY. Watch a child with a cardboard box and an old bed sheet and you'll see what I mean. However, children do appreciate spaces of their own—little nooks and crannies to hide in or rule over—no matter how grand or ordinary the space.

When you don't have an entire room available for play, take a look around the house and see if there are any small or awkward spaces that can be transformed. The space under a staircase can be outfitted with cushioned flooring and pillows; a built-in storage bench can become a window seat; a closet can be reworked to serve as a private hideaway.

Once you've found a spot, make it as comfortable and homey as possible. Consider including lighting, simple storage, colorful cushions or pillows, and framed artwork. It doesn't take much to transform unused space into a welcoming retreat. If you're stumped for ideas, enlist the help of your little one. He knows exactly what that closet-cum-castle needs to make it truly extraordinary!

▶ BUILT-IN STORAGE IN A HALLWAY makes for a private little hideaway. The seat was fitted with a safety hinge and transformed into a toy box. A little window keeps the area bright, while colorful pillows add a youthful, cheerful note. Attractive baskets keep building blocks corralled but accessible.

◀ A SEMIFINISHED ATTIC IS TRANSFORMED into an intimate playroom with the addition of rustic, vintage-style décor. Low storage cabinets and shelves give children autonomy, while kid-size furniture is right at home under the low ceiling. Cheerful yellow walls make the most of natural light, and a patterned area rug creates a homey feel.

# Transforming an Attic

Parents with small children are constantly looking for ways to make their home live bigger. Turning an unused attic or basement into a playroom for your kids is a great way to make the most of your living space. An attic can be the perfect spot for little ones, since headroom might be limited. The low, angled ceilings provide ideal locations for kid-friendly spaces, such as a desk or bookcase built into a kneewall. Because an attic is tucked away from the main living area it also allows more freedom when painting and decorating. This is a good place to let your kids be involved in the color choice and decorating scheme.

▲ ADDING A BUILT-IN STORAGE UNIT around the window creates a natural reading nook with space for more than one child. Underbench cabinets provide additional storage for books, while vertical shelves allow for colorful display storage.

▲ FORMERLY UNUSED ATTIC SPACE gets a makeover and becomes a bright and lively playroom with areas for floor play, theatre, and arts and crafts. Insulated flooring means children can run to their heart's content. Walls are painted in a neutral shade to make ceilings seem higher.

▶ A SLIGHTLY RAISED PLATFORM creates a natural stage for performances complemented by the architectural lines of the sloped ceiling. A painted mural adds visual interest to the low wall, while hooks and treasure chests offer costume storage. A convenient wall outlet allows for additional stage lighting or music.

▲ CLOSET SPACE IS MORE FUN when masked (and used) as a vibrant puppet theatre. The painted outline forms a strong focal point for the room, and the stage curtain is simple to construct using an old sheet or other fabric secured to a spring-loaded curtain rod.

▲ WINDOWS AND SKYLIGHTS BATHE THIS ATTIC ROOM with natural light, providing a cheerful backdrop for play. Built-in storage makes use of awkward space while baskets and bins keep everything organized on the open shelves. A cheerful wall border placed at kid-level adds a playful note to this soaring space.

▶ A SMALL BEDROOM WITH HIGH CEILINGS becomes expansive with the addition of a play loft built over the bed area. An open railing provides protection without blocking light, and a secured ladder makes for safe access. A small storage closet keeps toys stowed out of sight and the bedroom below clutter-free.

▲ THIS CHARMING PLAYROOM has all the comforts of a grown-up home but scaled for the small set. Coordinated upholstery and drapes make a vivid impact, complemented by bold red accents that create a stylish, unified look. Activity zones are placed around the perimeter of the room, leaving open space for floor play.

▲ HIGH CEILINGS AND LINOLEUM FLOORING make this half of a finished basement perfect for rough-and-tumble play. Mounted plywood covered with chalkboard paint allows kids to keep score or write on the walls, a classic childhood pastime, while treated wood paneling absorbs the impact of balls without excess vibration or worry about scuffmarks.

# PLAYHOUSES & HIDEAWAYS

► UNUSED CLOSET SPACE on a stair landing is transformed into a delightful hideaway, with a surprise porthole window providing outside light. The angled ceiling, while awkward for a closet, is just the right height for a young child. Sturdy footholds allow easy entry, and the hedges form a makeshift railing for support.

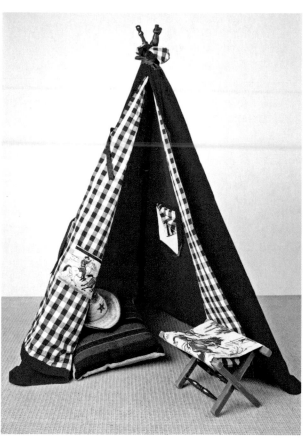

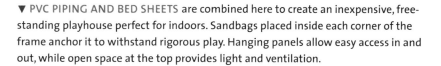

▼ PVC PIPING AND BED SHEETS are combined here to create an inexpensive, free-standing playhouse perfect for indoors. Sandbags placed inside each corner of the frame anchor it to withstand rigorous play. Hanging panels allow easy access in and out, while open space at the top provides light and ventilation.

▲ IT DOESN'T TAKE MUCH to create a personal hideaway, as evidenced by this portable teepee, perfectly sized for kids and easily tucked into the corner of a bedroom or living room. It's also perfect as a temporary place for shade in the backyard.

▲ A BEDROOM ALCOVE MAKES THE PERFECT SPOT for a two-story playhouse. A cheerful façade, complete with roof overhang and "porch" light, sets it apart from the rest of the room. A bolted ladder provides easy access to the second story, which houses a private reading nook.

# Activity Zones

To truly cater to children's needs, try dividing a playroom into activity areas, which creates opportunities for children to play together, as well as separately. Having different activity areas will also help when it comes to keeping the playroom organized, a must if it's going to live up to its full potential.

Game tables with low sides are great for train sets, construction sites, or dollhouses. Easels give a budding artist the option of painting while standing or sitting, and they keep masterpieces out of the way while they dry. A floor-length mirror and a trunk full of clothing are all it takes to create a dress-up area. Comfortable cushions and an overhead light turn an underused corner into a spot for reading.

Flexibility is also important in a playroom, where many types of activities occur. Consider installing two types of flooring and furniture, one to accommodate messy activities, such as painting or crafts, and the other to accommodate "dry" activities.

▲ AN INEXPENSIVE, UNFINISHED BOX fits conveniently at one end of a table, transforming it into an area for arts and crafts. Pull-out drawers keep supplies separate and organized but are completely removable for easy access. Drawers could also be painted and labeled, if desired.

▶ A CLEVER, HOUSE-SHAPED BOOKCASE easily divides a play area from a workspace while allowing visual contact between the two. A toddler can use the desktop for coloring or picture books while an older sibling does homework, giving them each some personal space.

## CLUTTER BUSTERS

# Incorporating Electronics

MOST CHILDREN, FROM A VERY YOUNG AGE, WANT TO WATCH TELEVISION AND MOVIES and listen to music. Instead of letting your kids hold your entertainment devices hostage, consider giving them something of their own.

If you include a television or stereo system in your child's playroom, think about placement. You might want to put the TV on a slightly lower shelf so that it's at eye level for your children, perhaps behind doors for a less cluttered look. But keep the VCR or DVD player on a higher shelf that only you can access.

A stereo system can be hidden away behind a locked cabinet, with speakers mounted in ceiling corners to keep wires away from little ones and prevent a tangled mess. A portable CD player could be docked on a higher shelf to increase its life span and keep it out of view.

Above all, keep it safe. Kids are curious about everything and will quickly mimic your actions. Keeping electronics out of sight and reach as much as possible will alleviate some of that curiosity and the temptation to touch—safer for the kids *and* the electronics.

► A CUSTOMIZED BUILT-IN houses the television in this child's playroom, becoming part of the décor. The television fits tightly in the cabinet, keeping out stray objects and little hands. The VCR fits overhead behind faux drawers. Movies are stored in bottom drawers for easy selection by kids.

# Super-Sizing Kid-Size Furniture

CHILDREN'S FURNITURE HAS COME A LONG WAY OVER THE YEARS. If there's an adult version, you can bet there's a child's version as well. Equipping the playroom with kids' furniture has its merits: Scaled-down pieces fit easily inside small spaces and are accessible and safe for your child.

However, the best spaces will incorporate a mix of pint-size furniture and larger-scale items that can be retained over the years. Children grow fast and you won't want to replace everything in the playroom every few years. Do consider a small table and chairs, some low storage or accessible rolling carts, and perhaps a small-scale reading chair. Balance those pieces with built-ins or large bookcases for adaptable storage and a larger loveseat, sofa, or window seat for television and movies.

Invest in the furniture that will get used the most; you'll get your money's worth out of a wooden table and chairs, but a plastic storage bin might be a better investment than a wooden toy chest soon to be outgrown. And do consider plastic blow-up furniture, such as an armchair. Its fun-factor appeals to kids, and it's a temporary, inexpensive furniture solution.

▲ A MIX OF WOOD AND OILCLOTH make this charming kid-size table and cushions durable for many years of use. Smudges and spills easily wipe off the nonstick surface, and the decorative print adds a playful note. Distressed edges keep the table kid-friendly rather than perfect looking.

▲ A SMALL WICKER VANITY topped by an oversized bulletin board easily transforms into a craft center. A vintage organizer keeps supplies handy, while a cushioned chair is easy on little knees.

▲ THE RIGHT FURNITURE CAN CREATE the feel of a playhouse within a playroom. Tucked into a corner with a windowed backdrop, the scaled-down seating, doll furniture, and a feminine table all set the stage for make-believe and entertaining playmates while an area rug serves to further separate and delineate the space.

▲ A WELL-WORN DESK becomes a creative center in a family room and is suitable for both children and adults. Grown-up supplies mingle easily with kid's supplies when stored in clear acrylic glasses. A desk mat decorated with stickers appeals to a child's aesthetics while it protects the desktop from damage.

◄ AN ALCOVE UNDER THE STAIRS gets new life as an enveloping little reading nook. Glass bricks allow for natural light, while a wall sconce is useful for nighttime reading. A fitted cushion and tons of comfy pillows make it a natural choice for a nap area as well.

# Storage & Organization

**W**HEN THERE ARE CHILDREN AROUND, inevitably there's clutter. A path of discarded clothing, toy parts, half-eaten sandwiches...ahhh, good thing you love your kids. But while it's not realistic to expect a clutter-free zone at all times, you can save your sanity by creating storage and organization that your children can understand.

Most children don't mind pitching in and helping during cleanup—they just tend to get frustrated when they don't know what to do. You can help by making sure that everything has its place. Pegboards with illustrations, drawer dividers, labeled stacking bins, rolling storage carts, wall hooks, and shoe bags hung at child level—they're all helpful for keeping toys and clothing organized and they're accessible enough for children to use. Start early by showing them a systematic way of cleaning up and good habits will become second-nature, saving *you* a great deal of frustration down the line.

## CLUTTER BUSTERS

## Keep It Simple

**T**HE EASIEST WAY TO HELP KIDS LEARN AND REMEMBER TO CLEAN UP is to keep the chore on their level, both in terms of where you place the storage bins and what they look like. If the bins are fun and recognizable, chances are good kids will actually use them. They don't need to be elaborate. Go through your closet or basement and recycle things you aren't using any longer—old hat boxes or wire baskets once used for incoming mail. A great way to get young ones excited about cleaning up is to have them first help you transform the recycled bins into kid-friendly containers with paint, old scraps of wallpaper, or fabric and ribbons.

► A CLEVER MIX OF HARD AND SOFT STORAGE OPTIONS make your child's job of cleaning up less of a chore and make use of overlooked space. If you recycle an old storage bin, be sure all edges are smooth and decorations are adhered tightly.

▲ PEGBOARDS HELP TEACH A CHILD to clean up after himself. Outfitted with hooks and pictures of what belongs on them takes all the guesswork out of where things go. It's a solution that's useful for any type of hanging object, including rackets and sports paraphernalia as they get older.

▲ FREESTANDING STORAGE UNITS and mounted shelving come together to create an attractive, organized space in a room without other options. A rolling toy cart is either a vehicle for furry friends or toy storage, depending upon your perspective. Reach-in bins are easily accessible for children, while toys requiring supervision are stored on higher shelves.

▲ THREE SEPARATE BOOKCASES CONVERGE to create one storage powerhouse. Personalized bins keep kid's items separate but accessible on lower shelves, while more delicate items are stored higher up. A small magnetic board mounted to the back of the middle bookcase is a handy place for reminders or temporary display.

▲ THIS ROLLING LAUNDRY SORTER with its deep canvas bins is perfect for holding larger and odd-shaped items, such as balls and other sports equipment. The labels, made from colored felt, leave no doubt as to what belongs in each compartment.

▼ TODDLERS ARE QUICK TO LEARN the meaning of "mine" and practice its usage regularly. Personalized storage bins cater to that idea and motivate children to put their toys where they belong. It particularly helps when children of different ages are sharing a playroom.

▲ STACKABLE STORAGE COMPONENTS form a freestanding cabinet easily tailored to individual needs, mixing open shelves with drawers and cupboards. For safety purposes, keep storage units low or mount them to the wall for added stability.

▲ AN INEXPENSIVE ROLLING CART purchased from an office supply store keeps building supplies from wreaking havoc. The clear drawers make it easy for children to identify the contents of each, limiting mix-ups of toy sets.

▲ AN OVERSIZE BOOKCASE works just as well for toy storage as it does for books. Nearly reaching the ceiling, it maximizes vertical space, while hardware mounting it to the wall keeps it from toppling forward.

# Around the House

The best homes (and the most modern) welcome children throughout the house, not just in their bedrooms, bathrooms, or designated playrooms. Comfortable family rooms replace staid, formal living rooms, emphasizing families who spend time together, even if engaged in separate activities. Formal dining rooms used only once or twice a year are scuttled in favor of eat-in kitchens or casual dining rooms used on a daily basis.

This new openness in home design reflects a realistic view of how families are actually living day-to-day. Floor plans and furnishings that embrace all members of the family are more harmonious than ones that create barriers: The goal is to produce a visual and psychic flow that offers a feeling of comfort and security.

Bridging the age gap in décor may seem daunting, but really can be quite simple. Use colors you love in durable finishes, add touches of whimsy that are playful rather than childish, and have enough storage options to keep your home from feeling like a funhouse. Of course, all ages respond to good lighting and ventilation, comfortable furniture, and open, uncluttered spaces. Finally, give everyone a little space for self-expression and individual taste and you've got a home that meets a multitude of needs.

◄ PARENTS AND CHILD ARE ABLE TO SHARE SPACE easily in this family room equipped with a kid-size portable desk suitable for coloring or other play activities. Built-in storage keeps adult possessions out of reach, while mounted shelving and decorative baskets in the alcove keep toys close at hand.

# Kitchen

NO MATTER THE SIZE, THE KITCHEN TENDS to be the heart of the home. Your children will spend a lot of time here, wanting to be close to you when they're younger, peeking under pot lids when they're a little older. It's here you'll talk about your day, create memorable meals, post kids' artwork, paper the fridge with memos, and touch base with your children as they run in and out for snacks.

As the kitchen is always a high-traffic area, you can maximize its potential by creating areas in which your children can play or work without getting underfoot. A bar area, kitchen table, island, or breakfast nook all keep children away from the stove or other potentially dangerous areas while hosting casual meals, holiday activities, and homework sessions. A drawer or cabinet can serve as storage space for art or school supplies, keeping materials close at hand but out of sight. If there's room, a small alcove can be turned into a computer desk, easily accessible for both children and parents and also easy to monitor.

▲ A SMALL WORK AREA for an adult or youngster was easily created in this kitchen by taking out a pre-existing cabinet and utilizing the countertop as a desktop. Storage space was created with overhead drawers replacing under cabinet lighting and a desk drawer installed under the counter. A mounted bulletin board keeps paperwork handy.

► A SEPARATE KIDS' CORNER with a desk and task light built in under a kitchen cabinet puts kids where the action is but not underfoot. Art supplies are stored in the adjacent cabinet for easy access and clutter control.

▲ MEAL PREP IS A FAMILY AFFAIR with a built-in play loft over the kitchen area. Children and parents are within earshot, while kids are kept safely out from underfoot. A large open island offers another opportunity for the family to come together without getting in each other's way.

▲ LARGE OPEN WINDOWS give a spacious feeling to this kitchen-cum-family room. A comfortable sofa, television, and computer desk make this a suitable area for family members of all ages. An old wooden trunk serves as a coffee or play table for kids while meals are being prepared.

▲ A BUILT-IN BREAKFAST NOOK is perfect for casual family and kids' meals. It's also a great place for kids to hang out while meals are prepped. The storage drawers under the benches let toys and kitchen supplies co-mingle without clutter.

▲ CHILDREN LOVE TO HELP WITH MEAL PREP AND BAKING. This low countertop is ideal to accommodate little ones; enclosed sides help to contain bowls, utensils— and mess! Be sure to include child-safety locks on any low doors and drawers.

## CLUTTER BUSTERS

# Creating a Communication Center

I F YOU'RE LIKE MOST FAMILIES, your refrigerator door is awash in paper—to-do lists, important phone numbers, reminders, messages. It's perfectly serviceable, but eventually all those important slips of paper simply get covered by new pieces, and you're lucky if you can find the door handle.

If you're looking for a better solution, the answer is as close as your local hardware store. Specialty paints such as chalkboard and magnetic paint allow you to create your own communication centers wherever you desire. Paint a rectangle on the wall and finish it with a store-bought frame or molding, turn a basement or pantry door into an erasable message area, or paint over an old mirror or tray. It's an easy, clutter-free solution that can free you from the tyranny of the refrigerator door.

▶ A BASEMENT DOOR treated with both chalkboard and magnetic paint serves as a handy communication center for a busy family. Artwork can be rotated and later stored or discarded; to-do lists and other everyday messages are easily erased.

# Bathrooms

ATH TIME OFTEN VEERS BETWEEN TWO EXTREMES: You can't get kids in the tub or you can't get them out. If the former is your particular problem, it helps if the bathroom looks and feels like a fun place to be. The good news is that the bathroom, being so small, needs very little to become warm and inviting. A splash of color, a few playful accents, and you're on your way to a more peaceful experience.

If more than one child is sharing a bathroom, equality can help keep the peace. Dual sinks, cabinets, and mirrors go a long way toward giving each child a sense of ownership, as do personalized robes and towels with hooks for each occupant.

If the entire family shares a bathroom, storage becomes a key element. Adult grooming products, hairdryers, and razors must all be stored out of reach. Installing an extra medicine cabinet or a lock on existing cabinetry is a workable solution.

Individual or shared, the best bathrooms are safe, cheerful, efficient, warm, and inviting—a pleasing solution for the whole family.

▲ THESE CARS AND BUSES ARE REMOVABLE, so they're not only easy to apply but easy to remove and replace as baby grows up and tastes change. Accessories like these are widely available and versatile—they can be used individually, in collages, or in borders in any room of the home.

► A PLEASING MIX OF PATTERNS AND TEXTURES makes for a kid-friendly bathroom. Hooks placed low on the walls allow children to hang their own robes, while the medicine cabinet mounted high on the wall keeps its contents safe from little hands.

▲ HIGHLY CHARGED COLOR and fun patterns welcome children into this bathroom designed expressly for them. High-gloss tiles allow for easy cleanup. Patterned tiles on the floor mimic an area rug and add a burst of color, as do the painted tiles on the walls.

# KIDS' BATHROOMS

▲ TWINS LOOK FORWARD TO BATH TIME with this tub designed for two. An expansive tub surround serves as play surface and storage area. The mounted safety rail inside the tub allows toddlers to get a firm grip, reducing the chances of slipping.

▲ A FORMER GUEST BATHROOM is remodeled to accommodate several small children. The long sink allows for more than one user, keeping territory disputes to a minimum. The rest of the room is vivid enough to appeal to kids but designed for easy cleanup with scrubbable walls and tile flooring.

# Make It Their Own

I T'S EASY TO OVERLOOK THE BATHROOM when decorating; it's a small room, less time is spent there than in other parts of the house, and it may not seem all that important overall. However, making a bathroom truly kid-friendly can make a huge difference in whether your child is happy spending time there, either taking a bath or learning to toilet-train.

Because the bathroom is small, it doesn't take much to make it a cheerful space. Colorful hooks and pegs on the wall encourage children to hang their towels or robes while a whimsical clothes hamper keeps dirty clothing off of the floor. Hand-painted tiles used as decorative accents can warm up a potentially sterile room and monogrammed or playful bath accessories such as patterned shower curtains and area rugs let kids know the bathroom is designed for them.

▲ A NARROW GALLEY just outside the kitchen is easily restyled into a kids' bathroom. The skirted tub adds a cheerful note to the small space, while a window with café curtains allows for natural light—important in such tight quarters. Kids wash their hands in the nearby kitchen.

▲ COLOR ACCENTS ADD A PLAYFUL ELEMENT to this simple bathroom. An old-fashioned claw-foot tub provides easy access for parents and easily holds more than one child, if desired. A freestanding vanity replaces bathroom cabinets, warming up the room and offering ample storage space.

# SHARED BATHROOMS

▶ MIRRORS PLACED AT DIFFERENT LEVELS are accommodating to both a toddler and an older child—and are an easy solution for a bathroom shared by adults and children as well. A painted stepladder serves as storage and display space.

▼ PLAYFUL TILES ARE SCATTERED in a confetti-like pattern across a family bathroom, bridging the gap between young and old. Multiple cubbyholes and drawers provide ample storage space for the whole family. Slip-resistant textured floor tiles help prevent falls.

# Childproofing the Bathroom

IT GOES WITHOUT SAYING THAT SMALL CHILDREN should be supervised in the bathroom at all times. However, you should still childproof the bathroom as if the children were going to be unsupervised. That means covering all electrical outlets and unplugging appliances not in use in addition to storing them out of reach. It also means storing medicines and cleaning supplies in locked cabinets or on very high shelves.

Beyond those basics, consider safety when choosing décor as well. Opt for slip-resistant flooring such as textured floor tiles or vinyl. If using area rugs, make sure they have nonskid backing. Rubber feet on step stools or chairs can also help prevent falls.

In the tub, grab bars help provide stability for children of all ages, as do nonskid mats or decals placed in the tub bottom.

To prevent scalding burns in the bathtub, set your water heater to a maximum of 120 degrees or install antiscald faucets. They regulate water temperature when there's a change in water pressure resulting from the toilet being flushed or faucets being turned on or off.

Finally, if very young children are using the bathroom, consider a safety latch for the toilet and always keep the seat down.

▲ STURDY FURNITURE IS IMPORTANT in a bathroom shared with a child; choose substantial pieces that aren't easily toppled. Adult grooming products are stored out of reach of small children, while the high wall ledge offers another option for storage.

◄ THERE'S ROOM ENOUGH for a family in this bathroom with its double sinks and medicine cabinets. The colorful tiles and backsplash make a bold, artistic statement in this otherwise formal, grown-up bathroom. Ventilating windows installed through the mirror further define and separate the space for double occupancy.

▼ SAFETY GETS LIGHTHEARTED with these frog-shaped nonskid decals for the tub bottom, while separate knobs are eliminated on the faucet, making it less likely for children to accidentally turn on the hot water.

▲ VIVID, SCRUBBABLE WALLPAPER and a tile backsplash disguise the messiness associated with kids' bathrooms. A small stepstool with a nonskid bottom is just the right height for little ones to stand safely at the sink.

► COLORED TILES are carried on in the bathtub area with alternating shades on each wall to add visual interest. A rainfall showerhead is perfect for a kids' bathroom: The gentle spray is less intimidating than a forceful stream when children are ready to graduate to showers.

# Choosing Bathroom Décor

**B**ATHROOMS GET NOTORIOUSLY MESSY WHEN KIDS are involved. Learning to brush their teeth, washing their hands, potty training...all make upkeep a constant battle. The best options in a child's bathroom include surfaces and textiles that are easy to maintain. Scrubbable wallpaper or tile back-splashes, washable paint, tile flooring, and vinyl or brightly patterned shower curtains help disguise the daily messes until you can get to the deep cleaning.

In terms of overall décor, starting with a neutral-colored tub, sink, toilet, and cabinets will keep the bathroom from feeling dated too quickly. From there, add splashes of color in the floor or wall tiles, area rugs, window shades, walls or borders, shower curtains, and kidlike accessories. Down the road, these elements can be swapped out or updated with less expense.

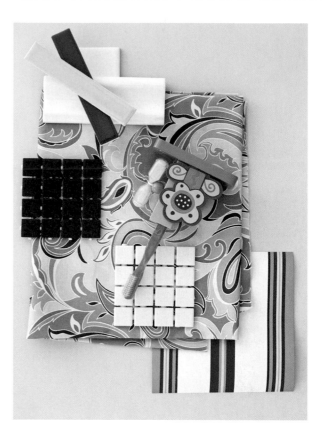

▶ ADULT PRINTS AND CHILDLIKE ACCESSORIES harmonize effortlessly when unified by color. Crisp navy and white are accented by bright bursts of yellow and lime green, an appealing palette for all age groups.

◀ WHETHER SHARED BETWEEN multiple children or children and adults, the twin sinks and shelves dividing the vanity into two sections help the room function well for more than one person. The tub/shower unit is on the opposite wall, creating zones that allow separate areas to be used at the same time.

# Family Spaces

WHETHER A FINISHED BASEMENT, A GREAT ROOM, or an extra bedroom, the best family rooms are those in which all members of the family feel comfortable spending time. They're also rooms in which family members can engage in activities together, as well as pursue individual interests alongside each other.

Casual, lived-in décor, cozy seating areas, good lighting, ample storage, multiple entertainment options, and a mix of whimsy and practicality bridge the gap between age groups and make the family room one of the most appealing in the home. At its best, it's a room that holds many possibilities: a space to read, watch movies or television, play games, do homework, create art, or just talk.

A great family room serves as a haven within the home. It's where we go to relax, to get away, and to connect, all at the same time. It's a tall order for a room but a worthy goal to pursue, since the ideal home houses a family, not just separate individuals living under one roof.

▲ GROWN-UP ART AND A CHILDLIKE RUG harmonize effortlessly in this room, embracing family members of all ages. The eclectic mix of furniture is comfortable and unified by the rug's color palette. The sofa, with its vibrant cushions, is inviting and appropriately durable for this high-traffic room.

▲ A BIT OF WHIMSY GOES A LONG WAY in a largely adult-styled room. Cheerful and fun, this alphabet grouping appeals to all age groups and makes the room feel more kid friendly while not coming off as a kids' room.

▲ THIS EATING AREA IS PERFECT FOR LITTLE ONES, offering room for a high chair to slide under the table, bench seating for baby as he grows up, and enough room for children to play without getting underfoot as mom gets the meal ready. Storage units with shelves and doors, plus drawers under the bench seat, offer much-needed storage for kids' stuff.

◄ A CUSHIONED BENCH is a perfect reading nook for mom and baby. This one, tucked into a stair landing, has protective railings on the side, keeping toddlers safe when they gain independence and want a place of their own to read.

# SHARED SPACES

► BUILT-IN SHELVING AND CABINETRY in a small alcove create a kids' zone. The cabinet top serves as an entertainment center, with space for a small stereo system and television, while a kid-size table and chairs offer a place for TV viewing or arts and crafts.

▼ SOPHISTICATION AND WHIMSY blend effortlessly in this charming room designed for the whole family. Decorative accents such as the umbrella lamp and muraled walls, with their Italian vistas, are playful but not overly childish. The elegant chandelier, sleek furniture, and rug balance but also harmonize with the more fanciful elements.

▲ THIS L-SHAPED FAMILY ROOM hosts a variety of activity zones for all members of the family, while doubling as sleeping quarters for overnight guests (and afternoon naps). Shelving visually separates the sleeping area from the more family-friendly daybed and desk.

▲ A WOODEN DAYBED WITH HIGH SIDES is the perfect spot for family reading and cuddle time. A red wagon stylishly stores stuffed animals, and kids' artwork feels modern and fresh in a formal grouping unified by color.

▲ KEEPING TOYS CONTAINED in a family room is easy with the addition of labeled bins placed inside of a low bookcase. Because the bins are easily removed, both access and cleanup are a breeze.

# ACTIVITY CENTERS

▲ YOUR CHILD WILL FEEL like she has her own part of any shared room when you enlist the aid of child-friendly boards to hang her works of art. Parents will love the creative—and inexpensive—decoration as well.

▲ PARENTS MAKE SPACE FOR KIDS in what was formerly a home office. Sliding doors with a window allow the office area to be closed off while still allowing for visual contact. Long cabinets provide ample room for toy storage and a dress-up area (the sliding doors can create a stage as well). Whimsical rugs can be moved around as desired.

▲ EXPANSIVE BUILT-IN COUNTERS are roomy enough to host the whole family in a work and play zone contained within a finished basement. Deep storage drawers accommodate plenty of toys and supplies, keeping clutter at bay. Mounted corkboard gives children space to show off their handiwork.

▲ THERE'S SPACE FOR THE WHOLE FAMILY in this comfortable room designed for solitary as well as family pursuits. Decorated storage cabinets keep games, art supplies, and toys out of sight while zones for work and study, reading or conversation, art, and floor play give everyone plenty of breathing room.

◄ A TINY ALCOVE serves as adult space in a family room. Shuttered windows offer natural light as desired and keep the area from feeling closed in. A long desk with two chairs, two lamps, and two drawers allows for double occupancy.

# Mudrooms

As children get older and families grow, coats, hats, boots, balls, rackets, bats, helmets, and backpacks can start to take over a home. The best solution for this ever-expanding clutter is a mudroom, whether a formal area or just a bench, hooks, and a coat rack placed in a front or back hallway.

A well-organized mudroom not only keeps dirt from getting tracked through the house, but it also keeps gear where you can find it and discourages children from dropping clothing and sports paraphernalia on the floor.

Locker-style cubbies, hooks, storage benches, and boot racks all work to keep gear stowed attractively yet practically. Vinyl or linoleum flooring makes the indoor area easy to clean, while a sturdy doormat encourages kids to leave as much dirt outside as possible. Durable finishes, such as semigloss paint or varnished wood, help as well, making your mudroom as mud-proof as it can be.

▲ IN A SMALL ALCOVE JUST OFF THE FOYER, built-in cubby-holes with attractive baskets provide plenty of storage for each member of the family without blocking access to closets. Positioned just under a window, the ledge is a good spot for flowering plants, providing a colorful focal point.

▶ AN INVITING FOYER AREA does double duty as a mudroom with the addition of a storage bench and shelving that feel decorative, even as they serve a practical purpose. Overhead storage and display space is an adults-only zone while wicker baskets in the bench keep the kids' stuff where they can get to it.

► AN INFORMAL MUDROOM is easily created in a hallway by placing a storage bench against easy-to-clean beadboard paneling. Mounted pegs are suitable for adult-size clothing, while the whimsical star hooks are placed for child access. Sliding bins in the storage bench corral small items, and a metal pail is repurposed to hold wet umbrellas.

▼ A BACK HALLWAY IS TRANSFORMED into a cheerful mudroom for the whole family. A wide window shelf offers plenty of space to drop things off, while drawers, cabinets, and cubbies both hide and display gear as desired. Stray dirt is grabbed by a natural, easily vacuumed sisal rug.

▲ A ROOMY MUDROOM replaces a formal entryway in this family home. Individual locker-style cubbies with adjustable shelves give each family member ample storage space. Whimsical hooks are charming yet useful. Overhead cabinets help with out-of-season gear. The dark slate floor stands up to heavy-duty foot traffic.

# Transform Your Entry

Y OU'LL BE AMAZED AT HOW MUCH STUFF babies and children require, particularly when heading out the door. Here are some tips to help keep your entry area organized and at the ready.

- Keep your baby's diaper bag full and in the same spot so that it's easy to find.
- Use baskets or bins to hold shoes and boots.
- Install pegs or hooks for small-size jackets and hats, since they easily fall off adult-size hangers when hung.
- Provide a bench or chair for changing shoes or temporarily storing bags when you come in the door.
- If you have a closet with a door handy, hang a shoe organizer on the back and use the pockets for winter gloves.
- Stash beach gear in a canvas tote so that it's ready to go when you are. Include towels, toys, and sunscreen.
- Install a hook for keys.

▲ A ROLLING BENCH WITH STORAGE CUBBIES contributes to a make-shift mudroom in a hallway. Baking pans make handy boot trays and can be stored under the bench when not in use. Colorful canvas drawers in the shelf overhead serve as a decorative element plus they're suitable for small, easily lost items such as keys, wallets, and cell phones.

◄ BUILT-IN SHELVING AND BRACKETS turn this area, located just outside the kitchen, into an expansive mudroom. It's an easy do-it-yourself option with pre-fabricated storage units and long shelves held up by brackets. Hooks screw easily into the underside of shelving, expanding the storage options even more.

# Resources

## Additional Reading

*American Baby* magazine
www.americanbaby.com

*Child* magazine
www.child.com

*Colors for Your Every
Mood: Discover Your True
Decorating Colors*, by Leatrice
Eiseman, Capital Books, 2000

*New Kidspace Idea Book*,
by Wendy A. Jordan,
The Taunton Press, 2005

*Parents* magazine
www.parents.com

*What's Going On in There?
How the Brain and Mind
Develop in the First Five Years
of Life*, by Lise Eliot, Bantam,
2000

## Websites

U.S. Consumer Product Safety
Commission
www.cpsc.gov
Contains a library of child-
safety articles

HomePortfolio
www.homeportfolio.com
Find products and design
inspiration

Get Decorating
www.GetDecorating.com
Design inspiration for the
home

## Professional Organizations

American Institute of
Architects
www.aia.org
Find AIA architects who do
residential work

American Society of Interior
Designers
www.interiors.org

National Association of the
Remodeling Industry
www.remodeltoday.com

National Association of
Professional Organizers
www.napo.net

## Product Sources

Babybox.com
www.babybox.com

The Container Store
888-266-8246
www.containerstore.com
Online custom planning,
storage solutions, and
products

Decorating Den
800-DEC-DENS
www.decoratingden.com

Glidden Paint
800-454-3336
www.glidden.com
Ideas, products, and color
consulting

The Land of Nod
www.thelandofnod.com

Netkidswear.com
www.netkidswear.com

Posh Tots
www.poshtots.com

Serena & Lily
415-389-1089
www.serenaandlily.com
Contemporary bedding and
fabric for nurseries and kids'
rooms

Velux America, Inc.
www.veluxusa.com

WallCandy Arts
212-367-8872
www.wallcandyarts.com
Peel and stick wall art for kids'
rooms

The Warm Biscuit Bedding
Company
800-231-4231
www.warmbiscuit.com
Bedding, furniture, fabric,
and accessories

# Credits

**Chapter 1**

p. 4: Photo © Olson Photographic, LLC; Design by Sheridan Interiors, Wilton, CT; pp. 6–7: Photos © Lisa Romerein; p. 8: (top, left & right) Photos courtesy Posh Tots; (bottom) Photo courtesy Land of Nod, www.landofnod.com; p. 9: Photo © Robert Perron; p. 10: (top) Photo courtesy Babybox.com; (bottom) Photo © Chipper Hatter; p. 11: Photo courtesy Serena & Lily, www.serenaandlily.com; p.12: Photos © Lisa Romerein; p. 13: (top) Photo © Lisa Romerein; (bottom) Photo © Wendell T. Webber; pp. 14–15: Photos © Lisa Romerein; p. 16: (left) Photo courtesy Serena & Lily, www.serenaandlily.com; (top right) Photo © GetDecorating.com; (bottom right) Photo courtesy The Warm Biscuit Bedding Co., www.warmbiscuit.com; p. 17: (top) Photo © Mark Samu; Design courtesy Hearst Specials; (bottom) Photo © Eric Piasecki; Mural by Lisa Williams at Welybom Studios; pp. 18–19: Photos courtesy Serena & Lily, www.serenaandlily. com; p. 20: Photos © Olson Photographic, LLC; Designs by Ramona Designs, North Kingstown, RI; p. 21: (top) Photo © Wendell T. Webber; (bottom) Photo © Scott Zimmerman; p. 22: Photos © Wendell T. Webber; p. 23: (top) Photo © Wendell T. Webber; (bottom) Photo © Scott Zimmerman; Design by John Loecke, John Loecke, Inc., www.jloeckeinc.com; p. 24: Photo © Mark Samu; Design by Lucianna Samu Design; p. 25: (top) Photo © Lisa Romerein; (bottom left) Photo © Mark Samu; Design by Artistic Designs by Deidre; (bottom right) Photo © Tim Street-Porter; p. 26: (top & bottom left) Photos © Mark Samu; Designs by Helen Otterness Decorative Painter; (bottom right) Photo © Mark Samu; pp. 27–28: Photos © Mark Samu; Designs courtesy of Hearst Specials; p. 29: (top) Photo courtesy The Warm Biscuit Bedding Co., www.warmbiscuit.com; (bottom) Photo courtesy Serena & Lily, www.serenaandlily.com; p. 30: Photo courtesy The Warm Biscuit Bedding Co., www.warmbiscuit.com; p. 31: (top) Photo © 2005 Carolyn L. Bates/www.carolynbates.com; (bottom) Photos courtesy Wallcandy Arts, www.wallcandy-arts.com; pp. 32–33: Photos © Lisa Romerein; p. 34: (top) Photo © Lisa Romerein; (bottom) Photo © Olson Photographic, LLC; Design by Ramona Designs, North Kingston, RI; p. 35: (left) Photo © Tim Street-Porter; (right) Photo courtesy The Warm Biscuit Bedding Co., www.warmbiscuit.com; p. 36: (left, top & bottom) Photos © Wendell T. Webber; (right) Photo © Mark Samu; Design courtesy Hearst Specials; p. 37: Photo © www.stevevierraphotography. com; p. 38: (top) Photo courtesy Serena & Lily, www.serenaandlily.com; (bottom, left & right) Photos © Lisa Romerein; p. 39: (left) Photo © Wendell T. Webber; (right) Photo © Lisa Romerein; pp. 40–41: Photos © Wendell T. Webber.

**Chapter 2**

p. 42: Photo © Olson Photographic, LLC; Design by Illustrated Interiors, Madison, CT, and J.W. Designs, Killingworth, CT; p. 44: (top) Photo © Linda Alfson, Architect, AIA; Design by Design Development, Inc., www.ddihome.com; Mural by Becky Le, Des Moines, IA; (bottom) Photo © Olson Photographic, LLC; Design by Illustrated Interiors, Madison, CT, and J.W. Designs, Killingworth, CT; p. 45: (top) Photo © Wendell T. Webber; (bottom, left & right) Photos © Mark Samu; Designs by Benjamin Moore; p. 46: Photos © Mark Samu; Designs by Paula Yedynak Design; p. 47: Photos © Chipper Hatter; p. 48: Photos © Tim Street-Porter; p. 49: Photo © Brian Vanden Brink; Group 3 Architects, 843-689-9060; p. 50: (top) Photo © Mark Samu; (bottom) Photo © Barry Halkin, Barry Halkin Architectural Photography; Design by JLJ Interiors; p. 51: Photos © Wendell T. Webber; Designs by John Loecke, John Loecke, Inc., www.jloeckeinc.com; p. 52: (top) Photo © Mark Samu; Design by Lee Najman Design; (bottom) Photo © Brian Vanden Brink; Theodore & Theodore Architects, 207-882-8492; p. 53: (top) Photo © www.stevevierra-photography.com; (bottom) Photo © Brian Vanden Brink; p. 54: Photos by Todd Caverly, photographer © 2005; p. 55: Photo © Tim Ebert; p. 56: (left) Photo © Brian Vanden Brink; Shope Reno Wharton Architects, 203-869-7250; (right) Photo © Phillip Ennis; p. 57: Photos © Wendell T. Webber; p. 58: (top) Photo © Brian Vanden Brink; Design by Drysdale Associates Interior Design, 202-588-0700; (bottom) Photo © Brian Vanden Brink; Sally Weston, Architect, 781-749-8058; p. 59: Photo © Brian Vanden Brink; Design by Drysdale Associates Interior Design, 202-588-0700; p. 60: (top left) Photo © 2005 Carolyn L. Bates/www.carolynbates.com; (bottom & top right) Photos © Chipper Hatter; p. 61: (top) Photo © Brian Vanden Brink; John Silverio, Architect, 207-763-3885; (bottom) Photo by Charles Miller, © The Taunton Press, Inc.; p. 62: Photos © Mark Samu; Designs by Lucianna Samu Designs; p. 63: Photos © GetDecorating.com; p. 64: (top) Photo © Brian Vanden Brink; Whitten-Winkelman Architects, 207-774-0111; (bottom) Photo © Brian Vanden Brink; Design by Polhemus Savery DaSilva, 508-945-4500 x14; p. 65: (top) Photo © Wendell T. Webber; (bottom left) Photo © GetDecorating.com; (bottom right) © Photo © Brian Vanden Brink; Barba Architecture and Preservation, 207-772-2722; p. 66: (top left & bottom) Photos © Chipper Hatter; (top right) Photo © Scott Zimmerman; p. 67: Photos © Chipper Hatter; p. 68: (top) Photo © Wendell T. Webber; (bottom) Photo © Barry Halkin, Barry Halkin Architectural Photography; Interior Decorating by Jeanette Samuelson; p. 69: (top) Photo © Wendell T. Webber; (bottom) Photo © Chipper Hatter; p. 70: (top, left & right) Photos © Wendell T. Webber; (bottom left) Photo © Art Grice; (bottom right) Photo © Mark Samu; Design by Correia Design; p. 71: Photo © Wendell T. Webber; Design by John Loecke, John Loecke, Inc., www.jloeckeinc.com.

**Chapter 3**

p. 72: Photo © www.stevevierraphotography.com; p. 74: Photos © Mark Samu; Designs by Lee Najman Design; p. 75: (left) Photo © 2005 Carolyn L. Bates/www.carolynbates.com; (right) Photo © Barry Halkin, Barry Halkin Architectural Photography; Design by Metcalfe Architecture & Design; p. 76: (top) Photo © Tim Street-Porter; (bottom) Photo © Alise O'Brien; p. 77: (top) Photo © Tim Street-Porter; (bottom) Photo courtesy Glidden, www.glidden.com; p. 78: (top) Photo © 2005 Carolyn L. Bates/www.carolynbates.com; (bottom) Photo © Ricardo Moncada; Victoria Benatar, Architect; p. 79: (top) Photo © Chipper Hatter; (bottom) Photo © Barry Halkin, Barry Halkin Architectural Photography; Neil K. Johnson, Architect, AIA; pp. 80–81: Photos © GetDecorating.com; p. 82: (left) Photo courtesy Velux-America, Inc.; (right) Photo © Jane Frederick, Architect; p. 83: (top) Photo © Tria Giovan;

# For More Great Design Ideas, Look for These and Other Taunton Press Books Wherever Books are Sold.

**NEW KITCHEN IDEA BOOK**
1-56158-693-5
Product #070773
$19.95 U.S./$27.95 Canada

**NEW BATHROOM IDEA BOOK**
1-56158-692-7
Product #070774
$19.95 U.S./$27.95 Canada

**NEW KIDSPACE IDEA BOOK**
1-56158-694-3
Product #070776
$19.95 U.S./$27.95 Canada

**NEW BUILT-INS IDEA BOOK**
1-56158-673-0
Product #070755
$19.95 U.S./$27.95 Canada

**TRIM IDEA BOOK**
1-56158-710-9
Product #070786
$19.95 U.S./$27.95 Canada

**TILE IDEA BOOK**
1-56158-709-5
Product #070785
$19.95 U.S./$27.95 Canada

**STONESCAPING IDEA BOOK**
1-56158-763-X
Product #070824
$14.95 U.S./$21.00 Canada

**OUTDOOR LIVING IDEA BOOK**
1-56158-757-5
Product #070820
$19.95 U.S./$27.95 Canada

**ORGANIZING IDEA BOOK**
1-56158-780-X
Product #070835
$14.95 U.S./$21.00 Canada

**CURB APPEAL IDEA BOOK**
1-56158-803-2
Product #070853
$19.95 U.S./$27.95 Canada

**TAUNTON'S HOME STORAGE IDEA BOOK**
1-56158-676-5
Product #070758
$19.95 U.S./$27.95 Canada

**TAUNTON'S FAMILY HOME IDEA BOOK**
1-56158-729-X
Product #070789
$19.95 U.S./$27.95 Canada

**TAUNTON'S HOME WORKSPACE IDEA BOOK**
ISBN 1-56158-701-X
Product #070783
$19.95 U.S./$27.95 Canada

**BACKYARD IDEA BOOK**
1-56158-667-6
Product #070749
$19.95 U.S./$27.95 Canada

**POOL IDEA BOOK**
1-56158-764-8
Product #070825
$19.95 U.S./$27.95 Canada

**DECK & PATIO IDEA BOOK**
1-56158-639-0
Product #070718
$19.95 U.S./$27.95 Canada

**TAUNTON'S FRONT YARD IDEA BOOK**
1-56158-519-X
Product #070621
$19.95 U.S./$27.95 Canada

**FOR MORE INFORMATION VISIT OUR WEBSITE AT www.taunton.com**